George F. Watts:
122 Paintings and Drawings

By Maria Tsaneva

First Edition

*****

George F. Watts: 122 Paintings and Drawings
*****

Foreword

George Frederic Watts (1817 – 1904) was a popular English Victorian painter and sculptor associated with the Symbolist movement. Watts became famous in his lifetime for his allegorical works, such as Hope and Love and Life. These paintings were intended to form part of an epic symbolic cycle called the "House of Life", in which the emotions and aspirations of life would all be represented in a universal symbolic language.

He was born in London, the son of a piano maker. Initially, he wanted to become a sculptor, and at the age of 10 was apprenticed to William Behnes. However, in 1835, at the age of 18, he went to the RA Schools, where he remained for only a short period, and thereafter was mainly self-taught. After he first exhibited The Wounded Heron at the Royal Academy, painting became his main preoccupation. When his picture Caractacus won a prize, he used the money to finance a trip to Italy, where he stayed with friends in Florence. He did not return to England until 1847, when his painting Alfred won the first prize in a House of Lords competition.

In 1850 Watts visited the home of Valentine Prinsep's parents, supposedly for a three-day visit, but instead he stayed for thirty years. The Prinseps gave them a certain status in the Bohemian circles in which they moved, which included such writers and painters as Thackeray, Dickens, Rossetti and Burne-Jones. Watts flourished in this household, where notable writers and painters were treated with reverence.

As a portrait artist, his gallery of eminent Victorians is unsurpassed: included among his sitters were the poets Tennyson, Swinburne and Browning, the artists Millais, Lord Leighton, Walter Crane and Burne-Jones; others were Sir Richard Burton, John Stuart Mill and Garibaldi.

He finally left the Prinseps' home in 1875 and moved to the Isle of Wight. In 1864 Watts married the actress Ellen Terry, who was only 16, although the marriage was short-lived, and he remarried in 1886. His new wife was Mary Fraser-Tytler, thirty-two year his junior. She was of Scottish descent and was an artist in her own right.

Watts was a hard-working artist who twice refused a baronetcy and other honours, including an offer to become president of the Royal Academy. His declared aims were clear: to paint pictures that appealed 'to the intellect and refined emotions rather than the senses': "I paint ideas, not things. I paint primarily because I have something to say, and since the gift of eloquent language has been denied to me, I use painting; my intention is not so much to paint pictures which shall please the eye, as to suggest great thoughts which shall speak to the imagination and to the heart and arouse all that is best and noblest in humanity."

One his contemporary admirer, Hugh MacMillan, wrote that Watts "surrounds his ideal forms with a misty or cloudy atmosphere for the purpose of showing that they are visionary or ideal.... His colours, like the colour of the veils of the ancient tabernacle, like the hues of the jewelled walls of the New Jerusalem, are invested with a parabolic significance.... To the commonest hues he gives a tone beyond their ordinary power... Watts is essentially the prophet. He thinks in pictures that come before the inward eye spontaneously and assume a definite form almost without any effort of consciousness."

Since the revival of interest in Victorian painting, Watts may be regaining the recognition and respect he enjoyed in the 19th century. However, in terms of public recognition he is not as well-known as contemporaries like Dante Gabriel Rossetti and Edward Burne-Jones.

Paintings and Drawings

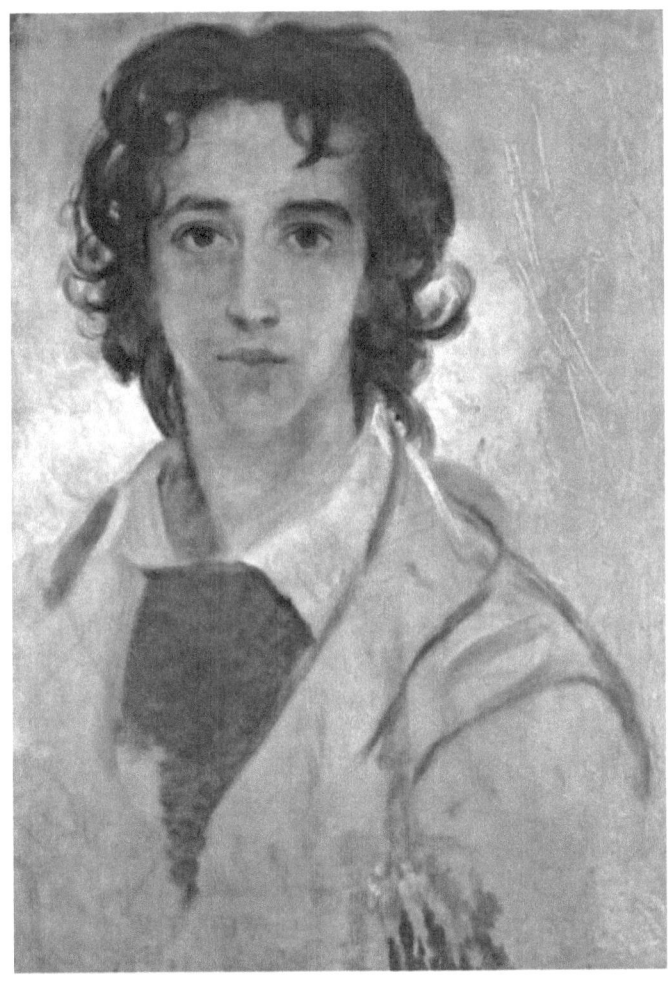

Self-Portrait as a Young Man, 1834
Oil on canvas

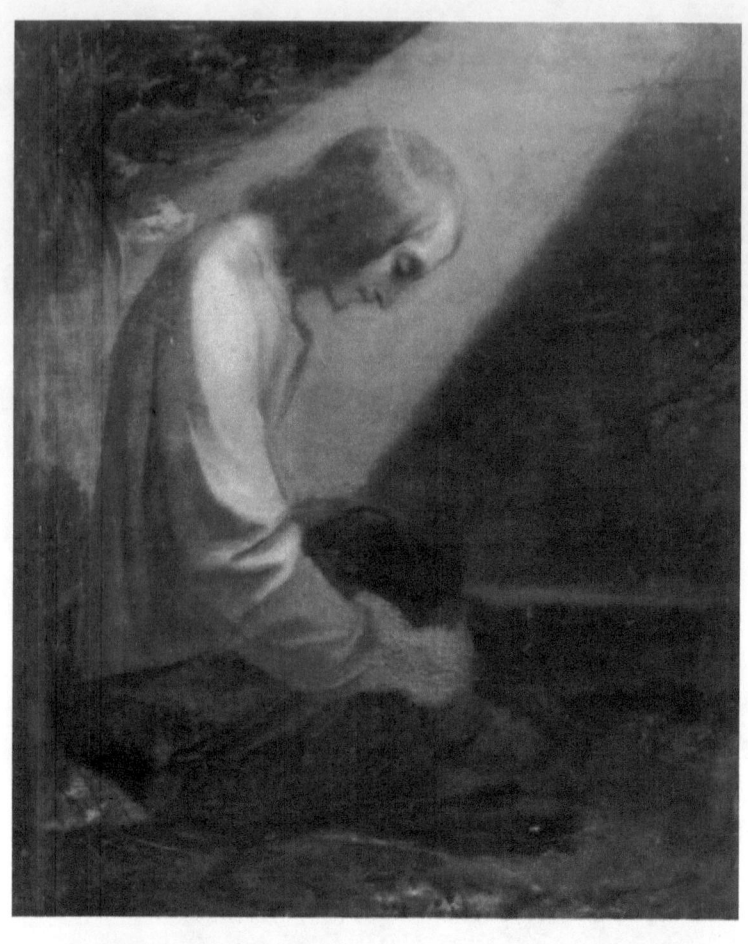

A Kneeling Figure (A Man of Sorrows), 1835
Oil on canvas

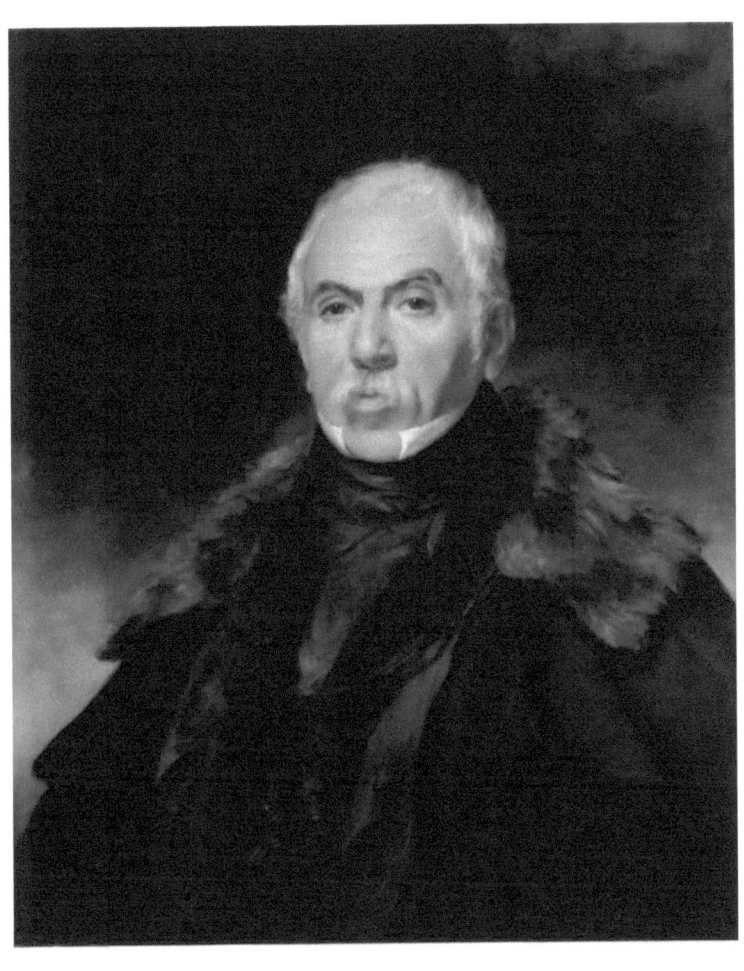

Constantine Ionides (after Samuel Lane), 1840
Oil on canvas

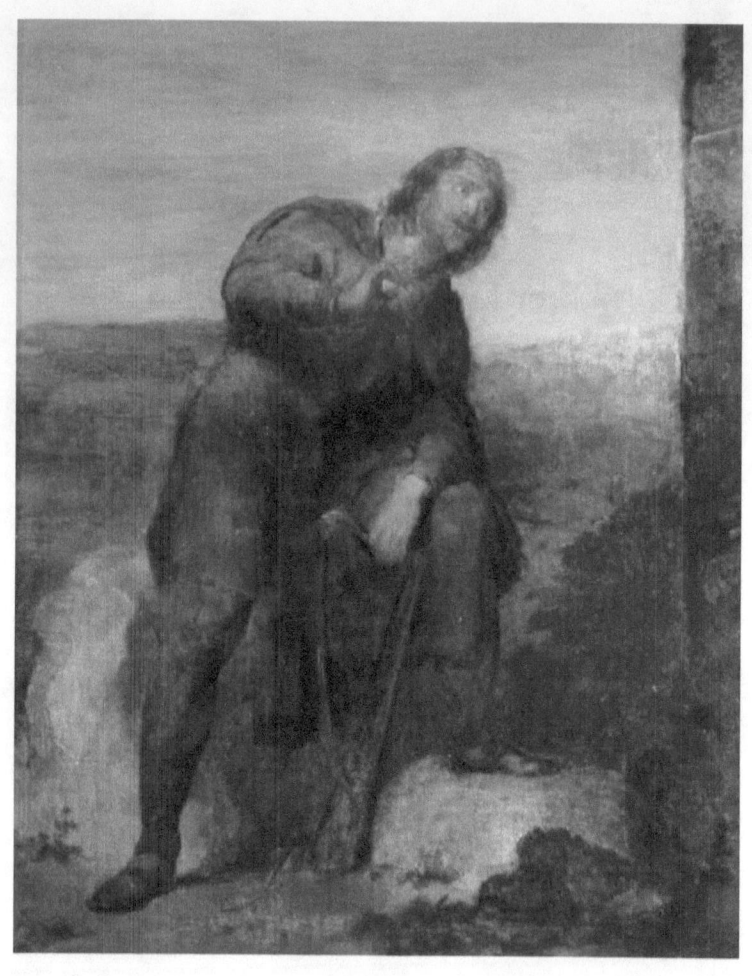

Blondel, 1841

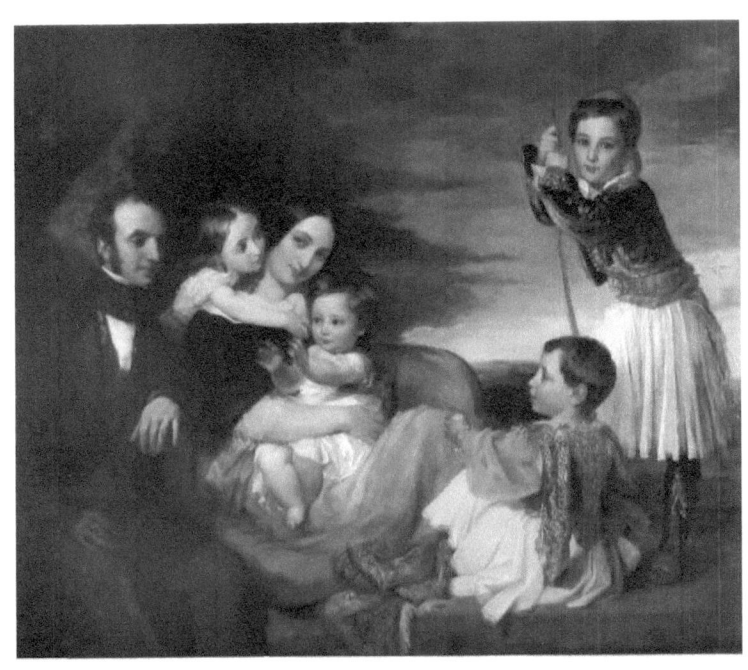

Alexander Constantine Ionides with His Wife and
Children, 1842
Oil on canvas

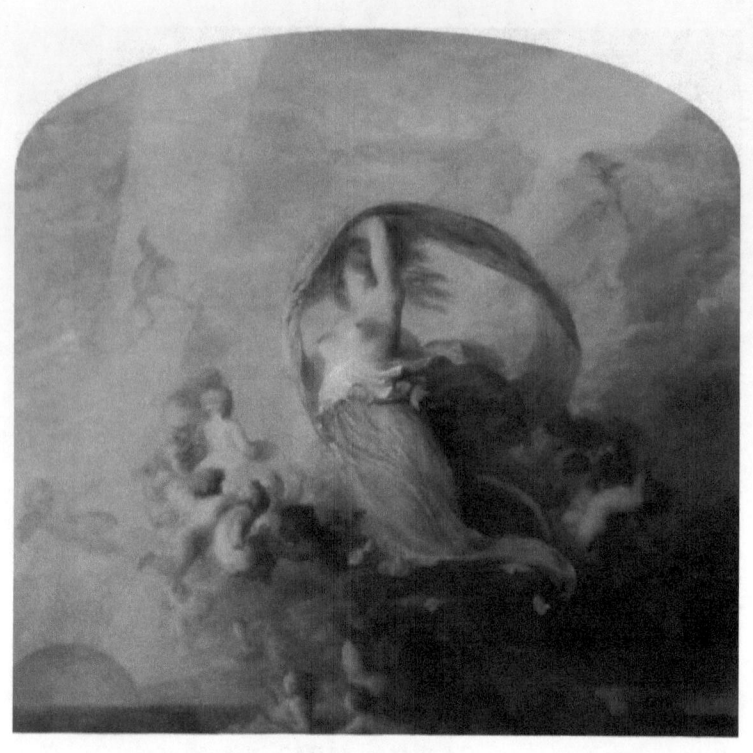

Aurora, 1842
Oil on canvas

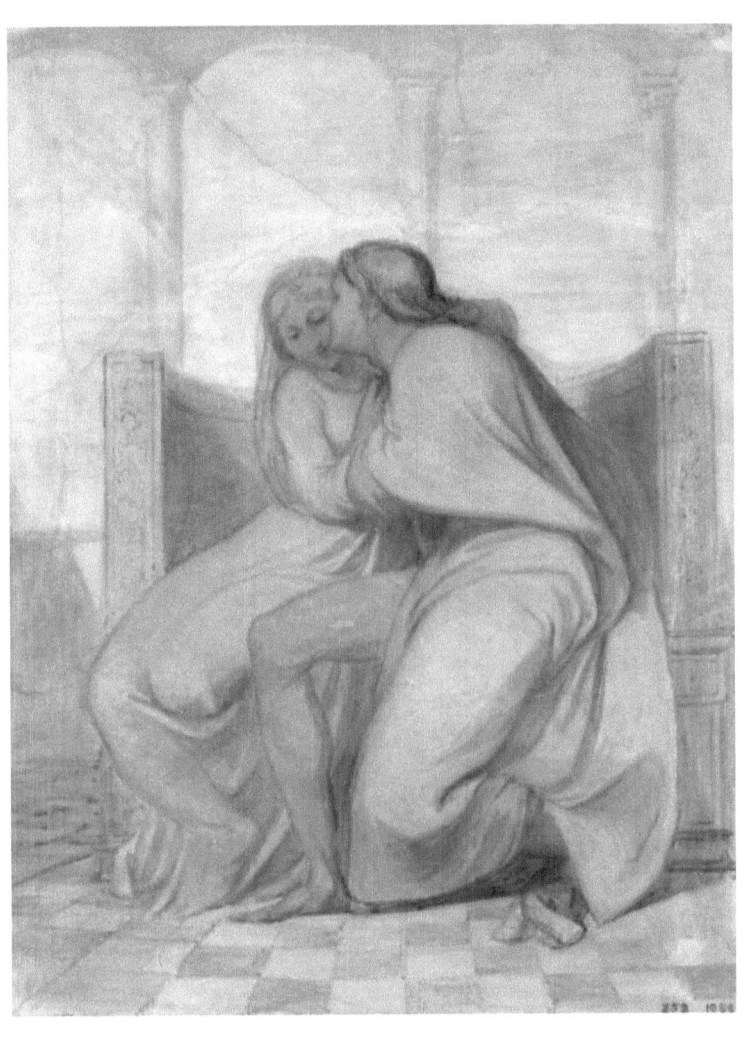

A Youth Embracing a Girl (sketch for a mural in the Villa Carreggi), 1845
Fresco

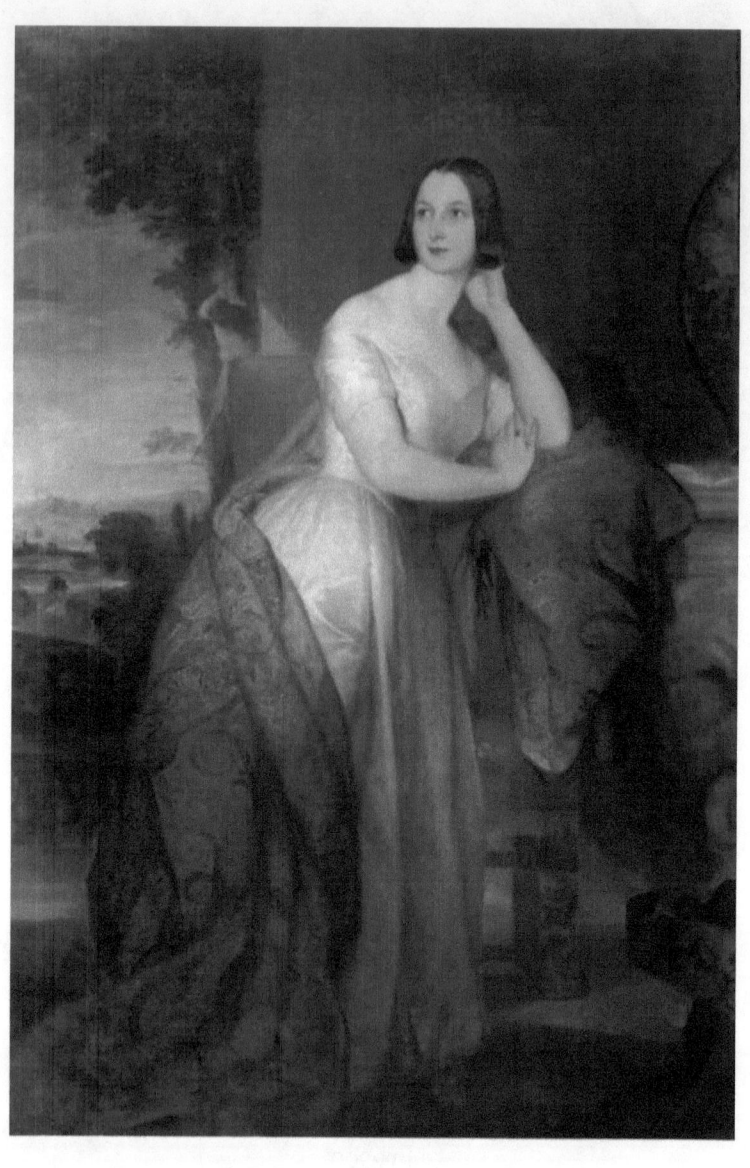

Augusta, Lady Castletown, 1846
Oil on canvas

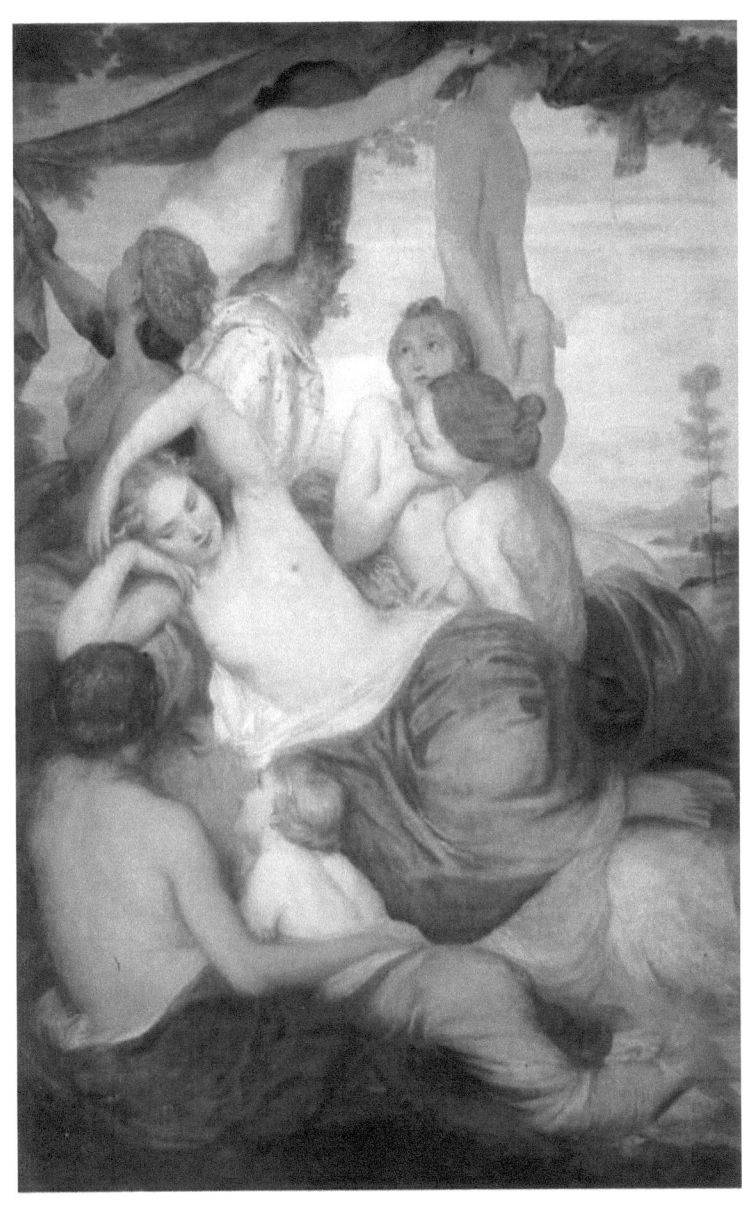

Diana's Nymphs, 1846
Oil on canvas

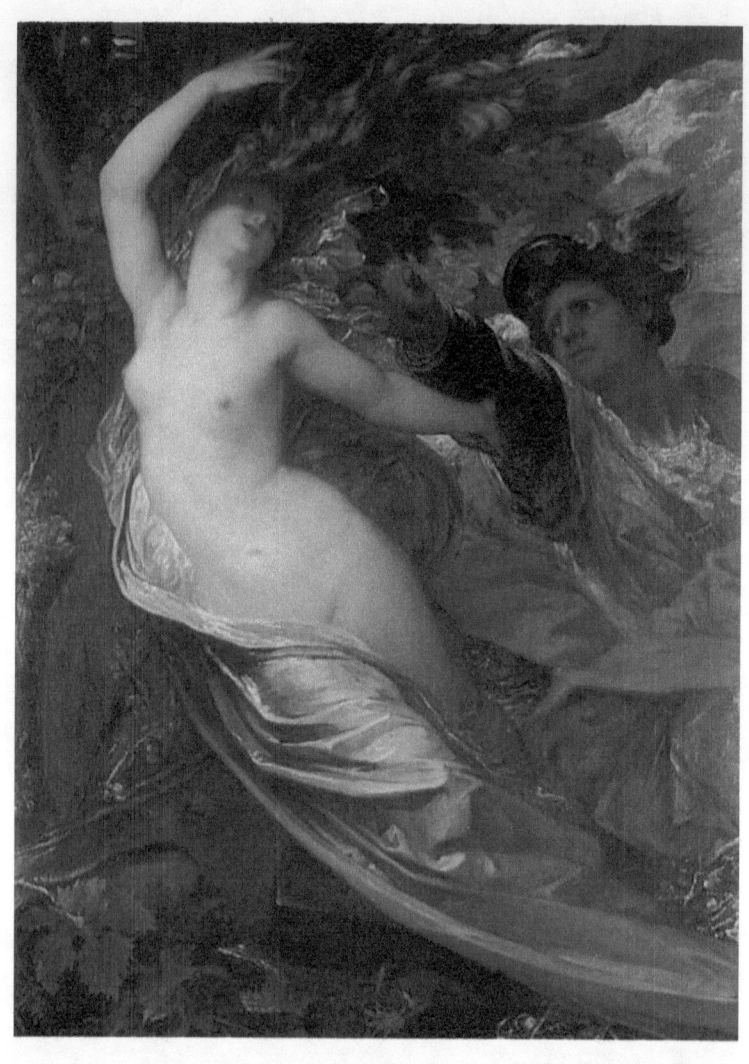

Orlando Pursuing the Fata Morgana, 1846-1848
Oil on canvas

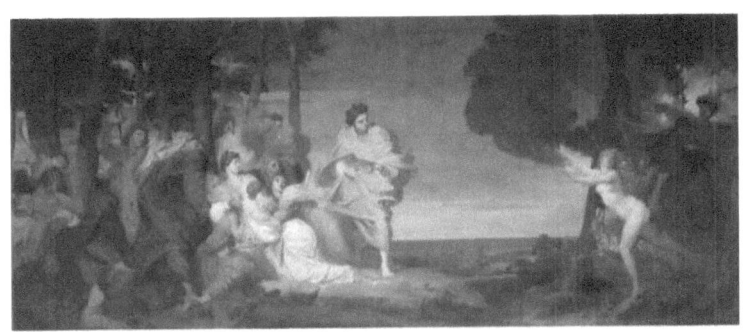

A Story from Boccaccio, 1847
Oil on canvas

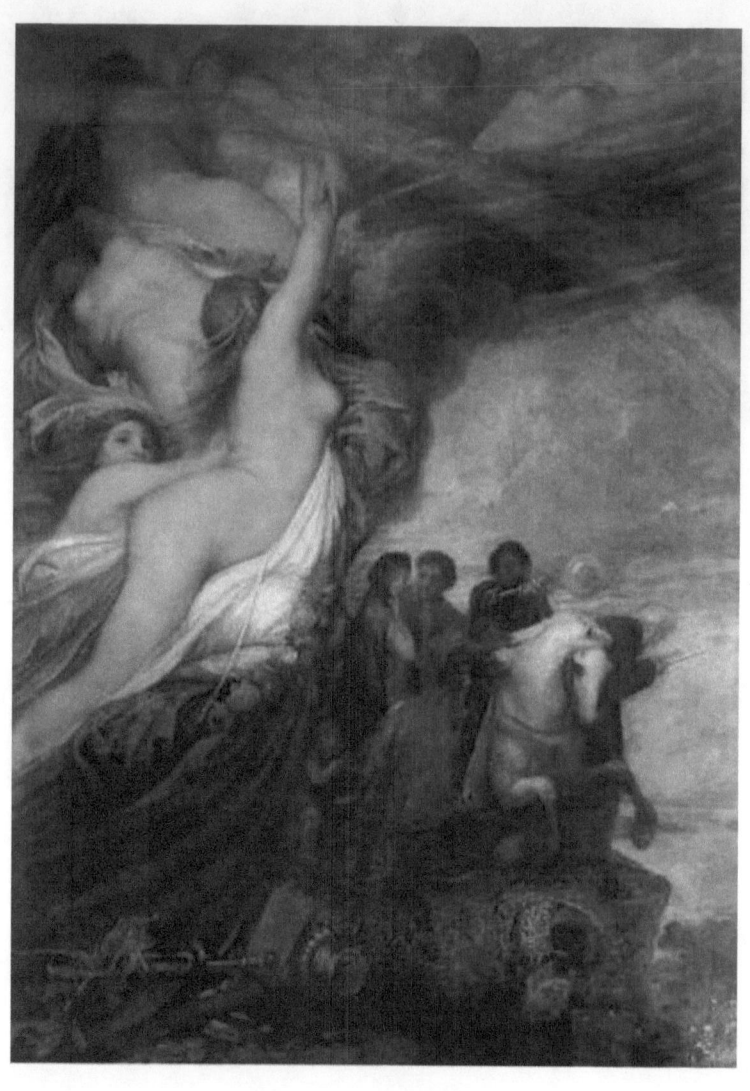

Life's Illusions, 1849
Oil on canvas

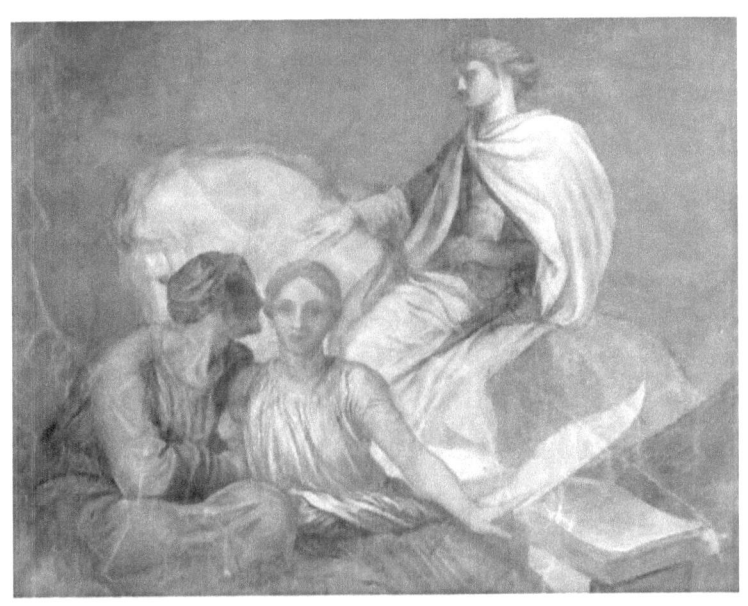

Britomart, 1850
Fresco

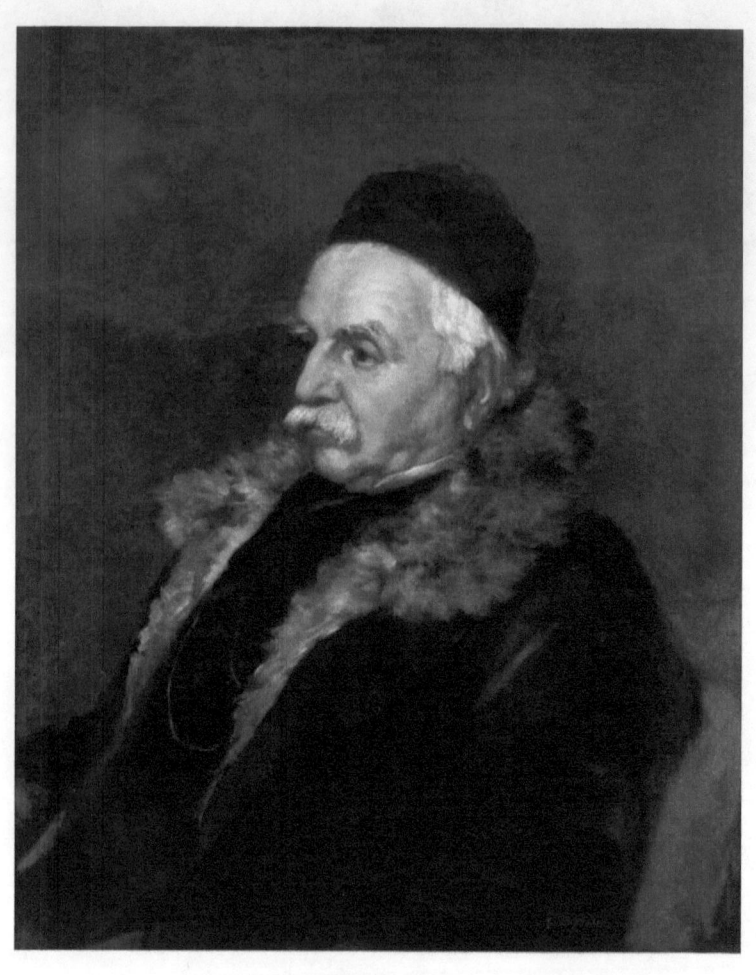

Constantine John Ionides, 1850
Oil on canvas

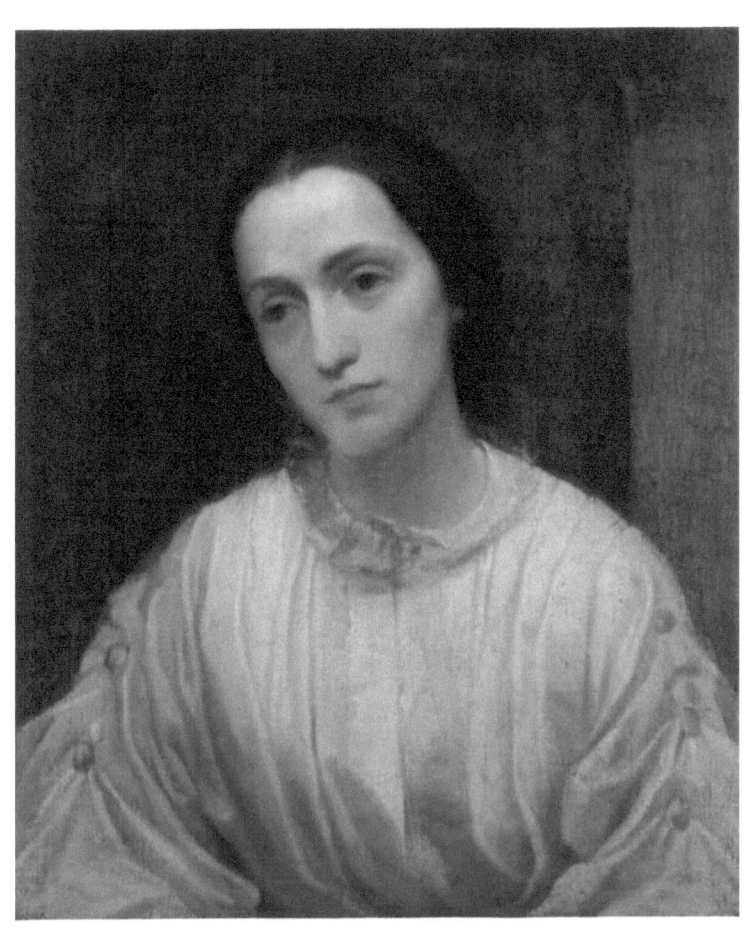

Julia Margaret Cameron, 1850-1852
Oil on canvas

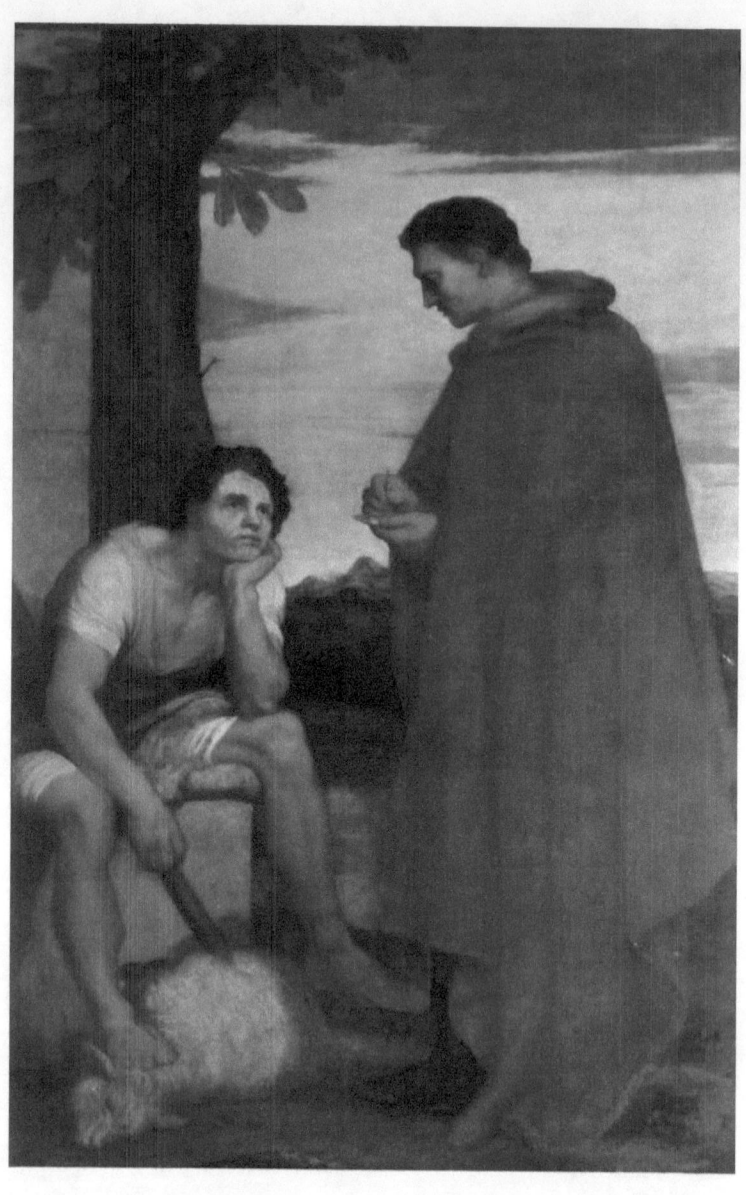

Aristides and the Shepherd, 1852
Oil on canvas

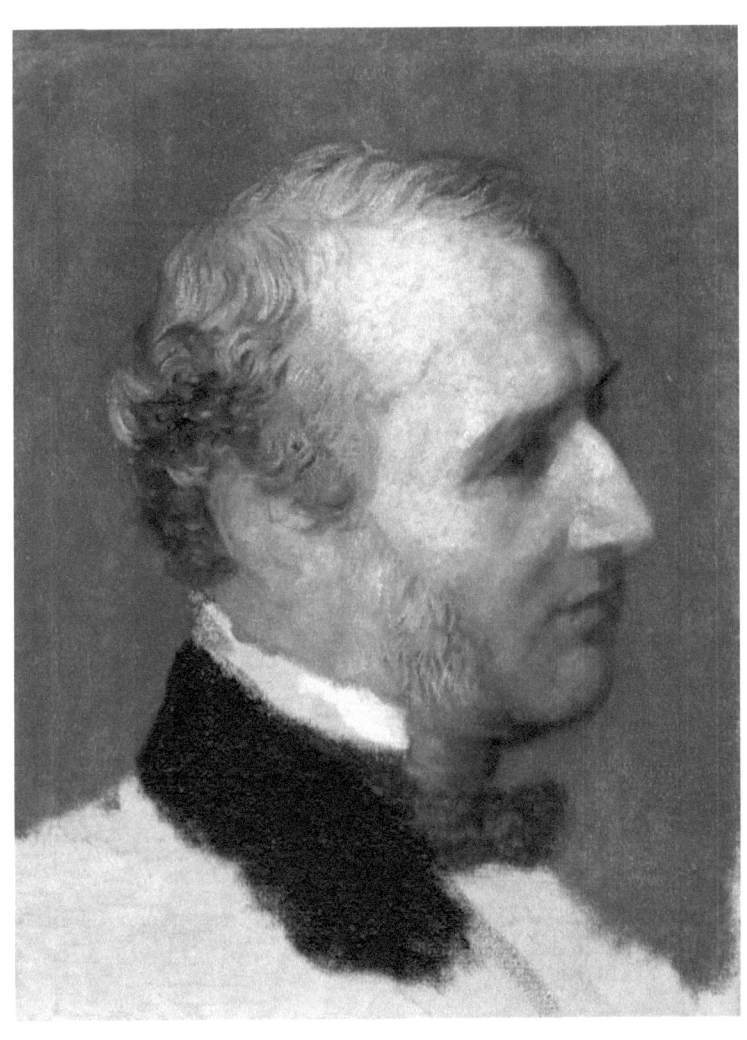

Carlo, Baron Marochetti, 1852
Oil on canvas

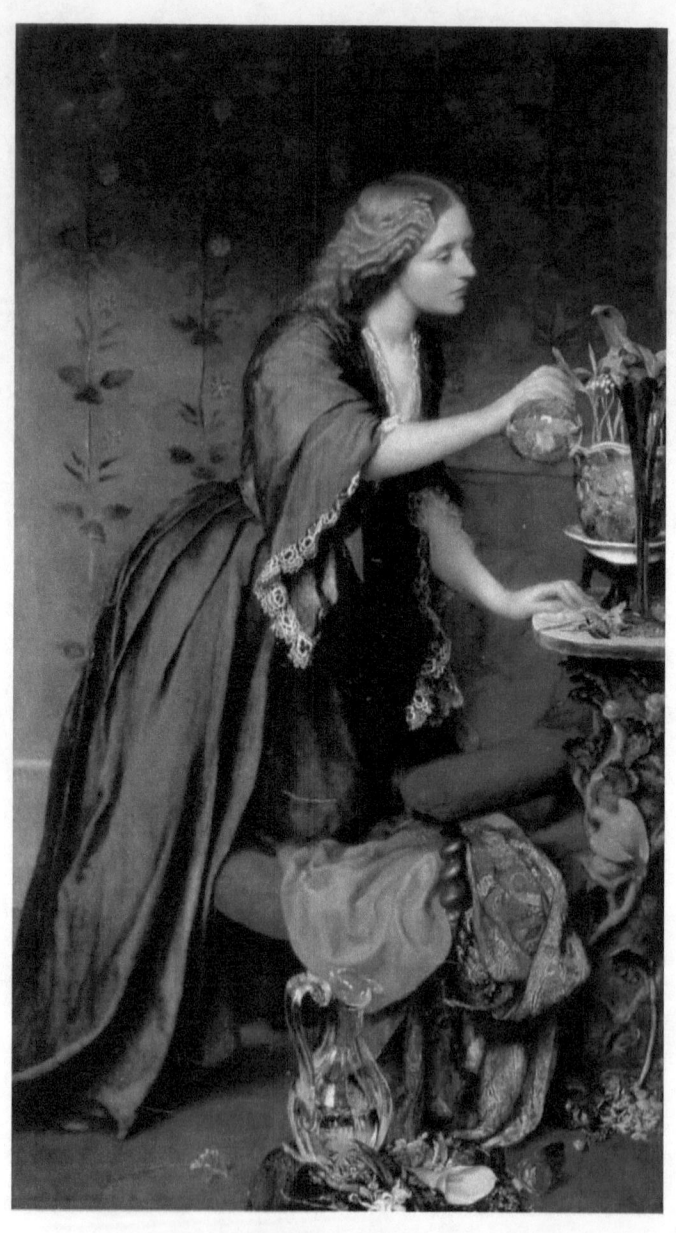

Jane Senior, 1857-1858
Oil on canvas

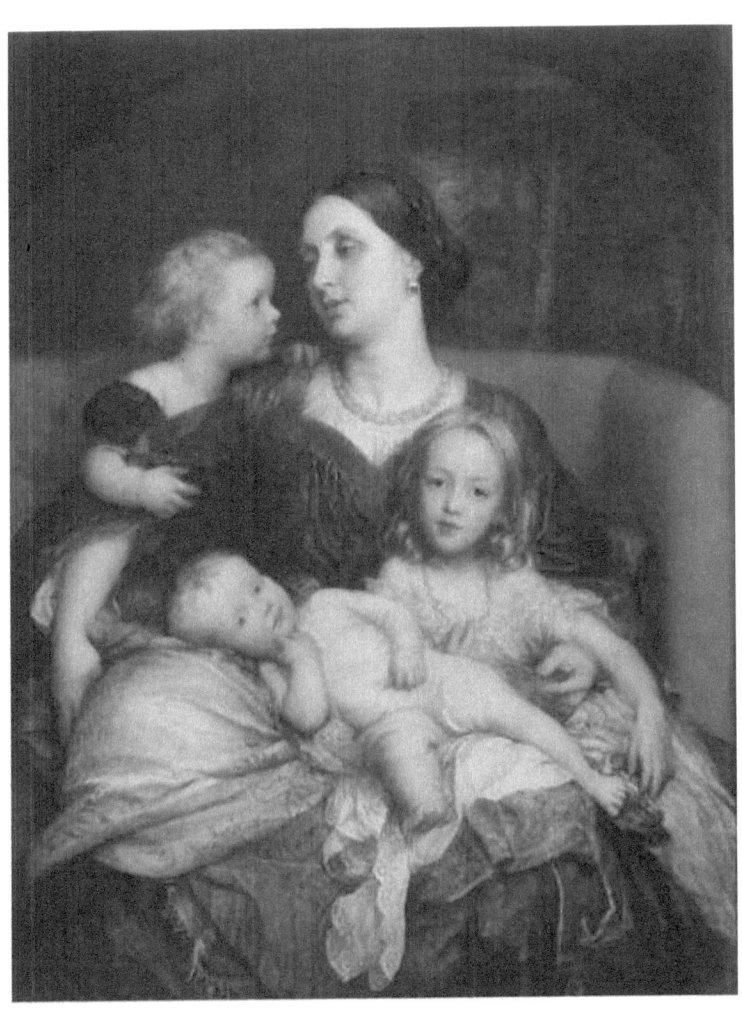

Mrs George Augustus Frederick Cavendish Bentinck
and her Children, 1860
Oil on canvas

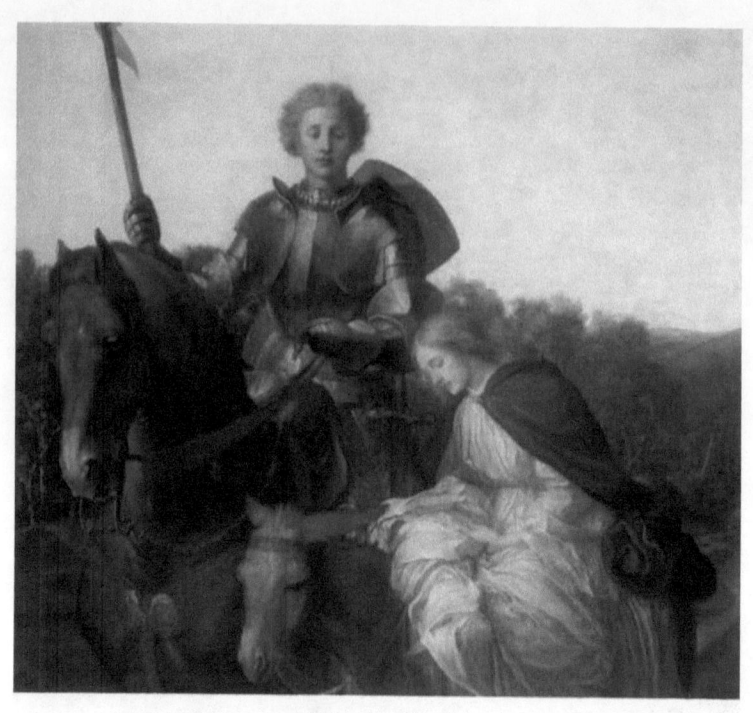

Una and the Red Cross Knight, 1860
Oil on canvas

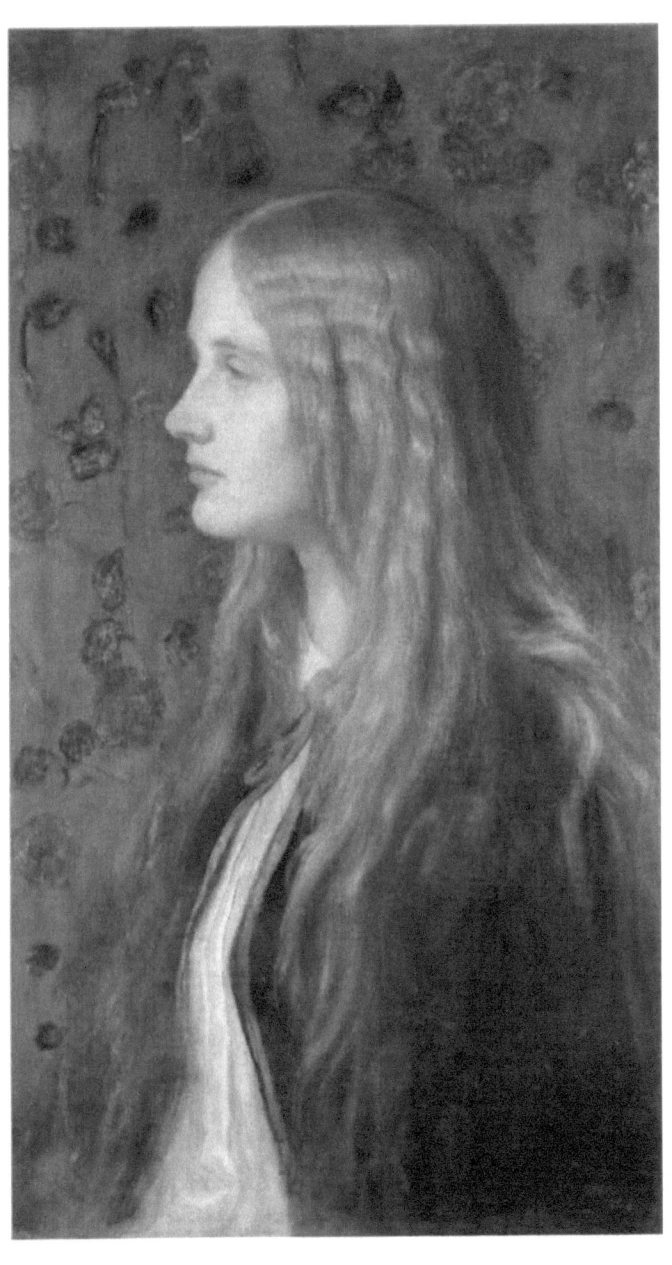

Edith Villiers, later Countess of Lytton, 1862
Oil on canvas

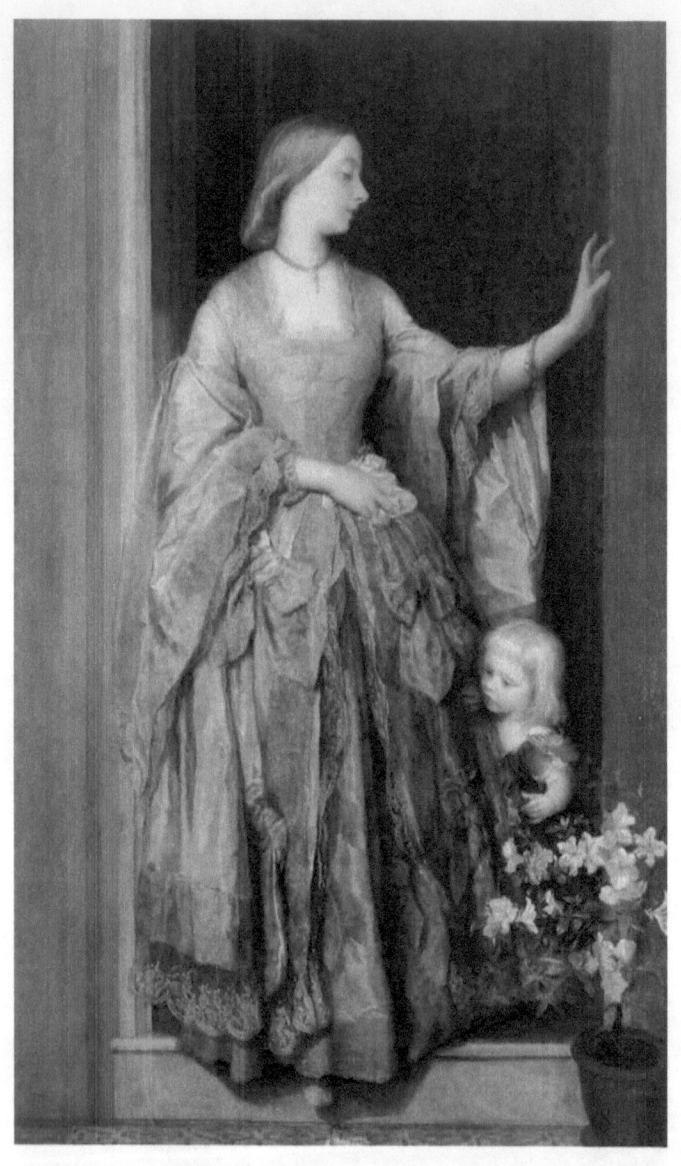

Lady Margaret Beaumont and her Daughter, 1862
Oil on canvas

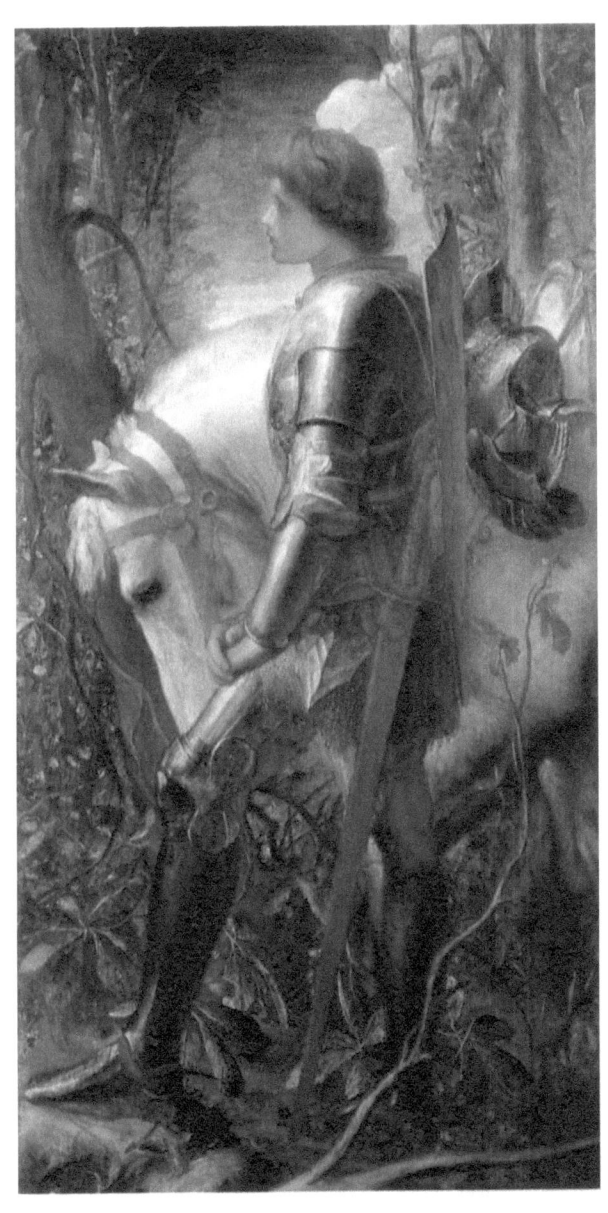

Sir Galahad, 1862
Oil on canvas

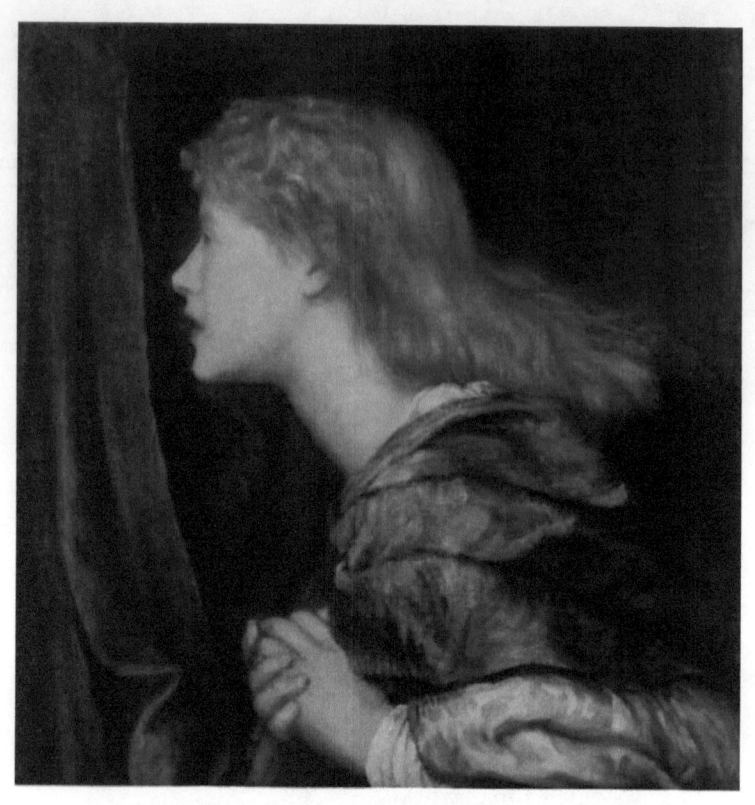

Dame (Alice) Ellen Terry, 1864
Oil on canvas

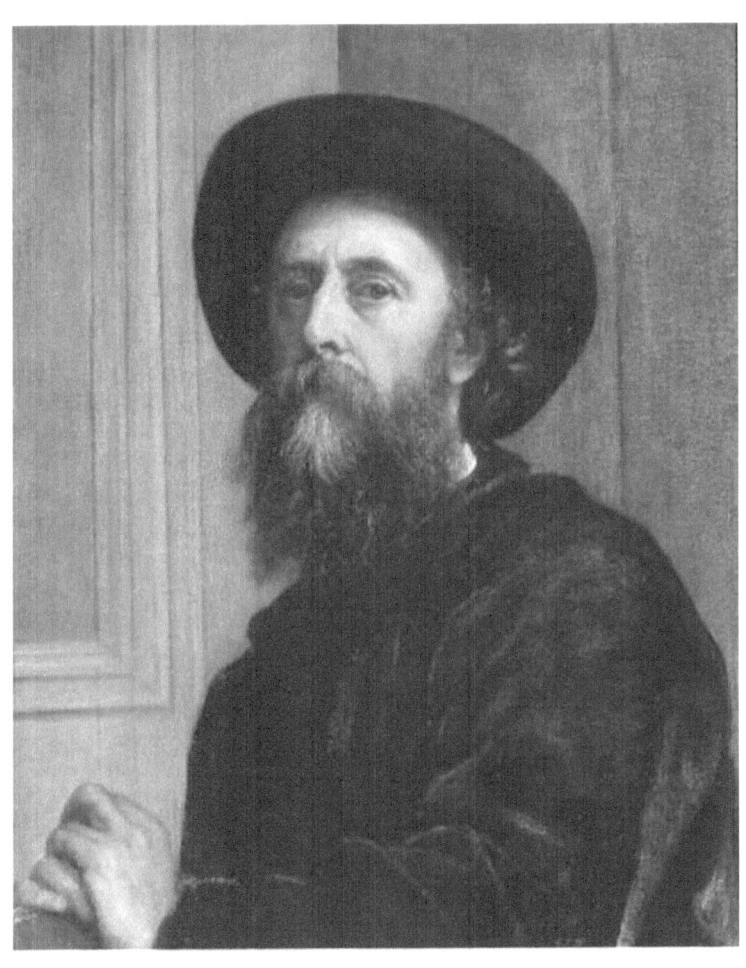

Self-Portrait, 1864
Oil on canvas

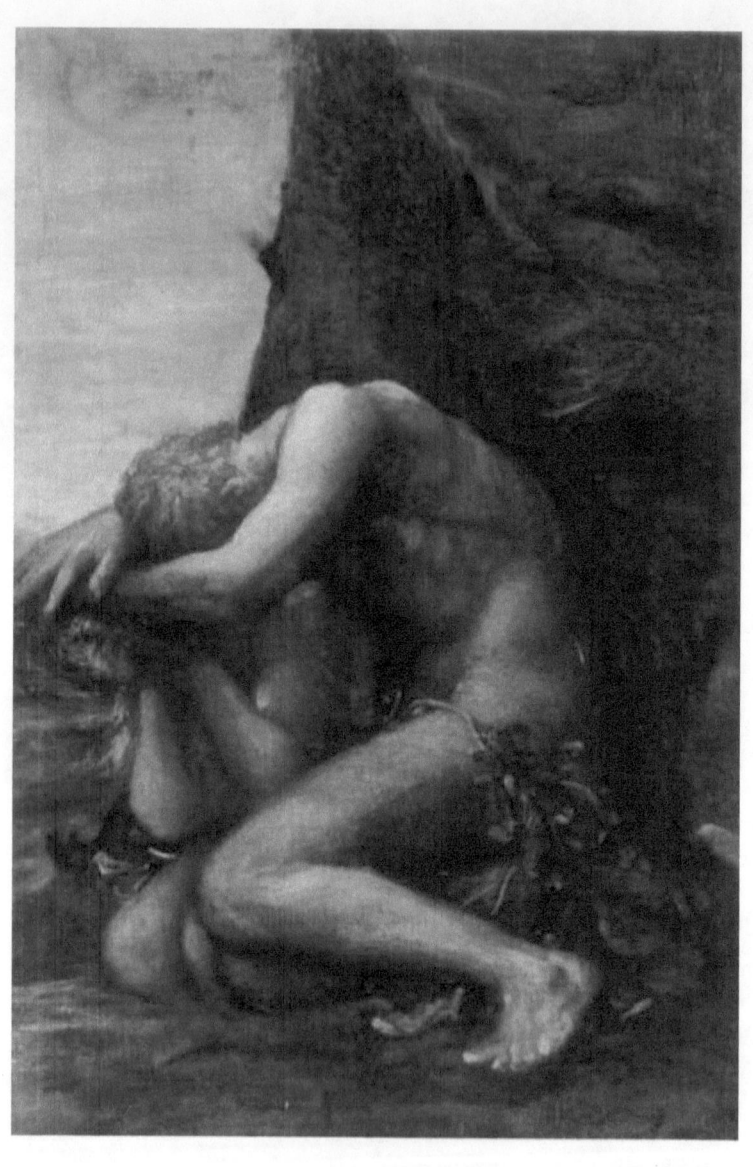

Adam and Eve, 1865
Oil on canvas

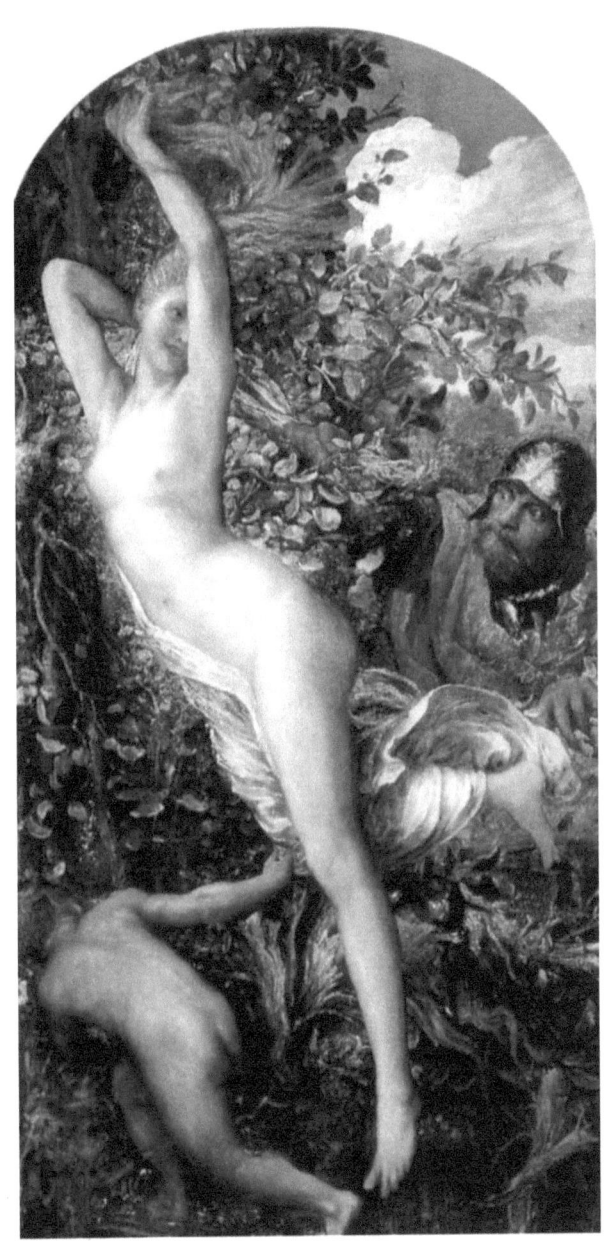

Fata Morgana, 1865
Oil on canvas

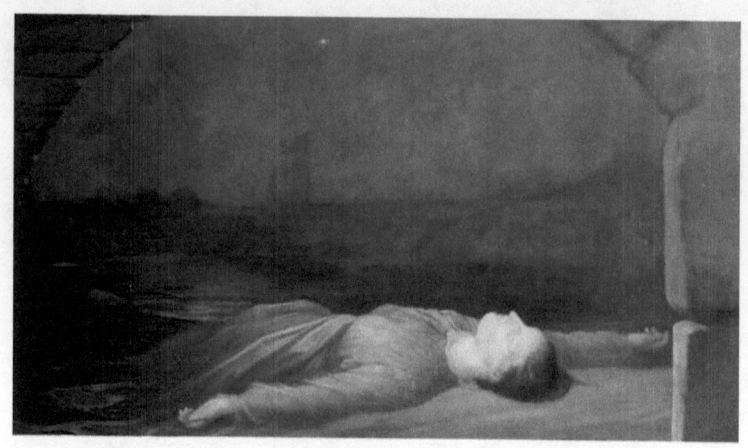

Found Drowned, 1867
Oil on canvas

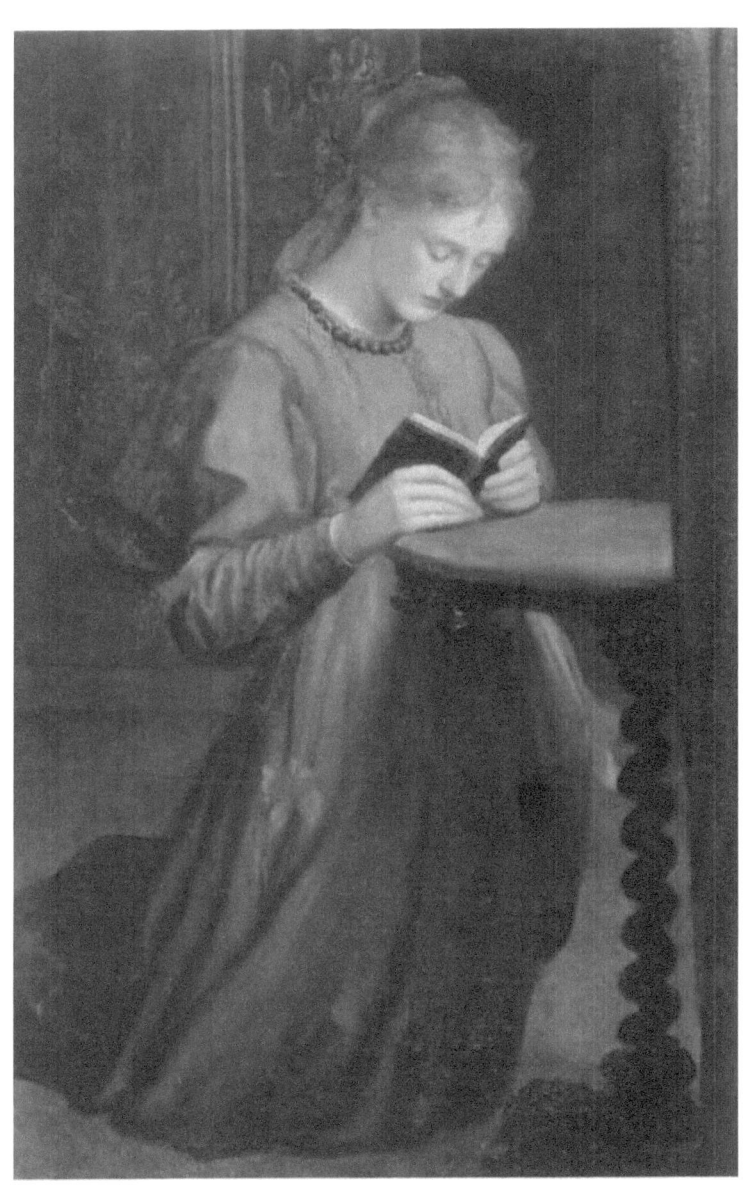

May Prinsep, 1867
Oil on canvas

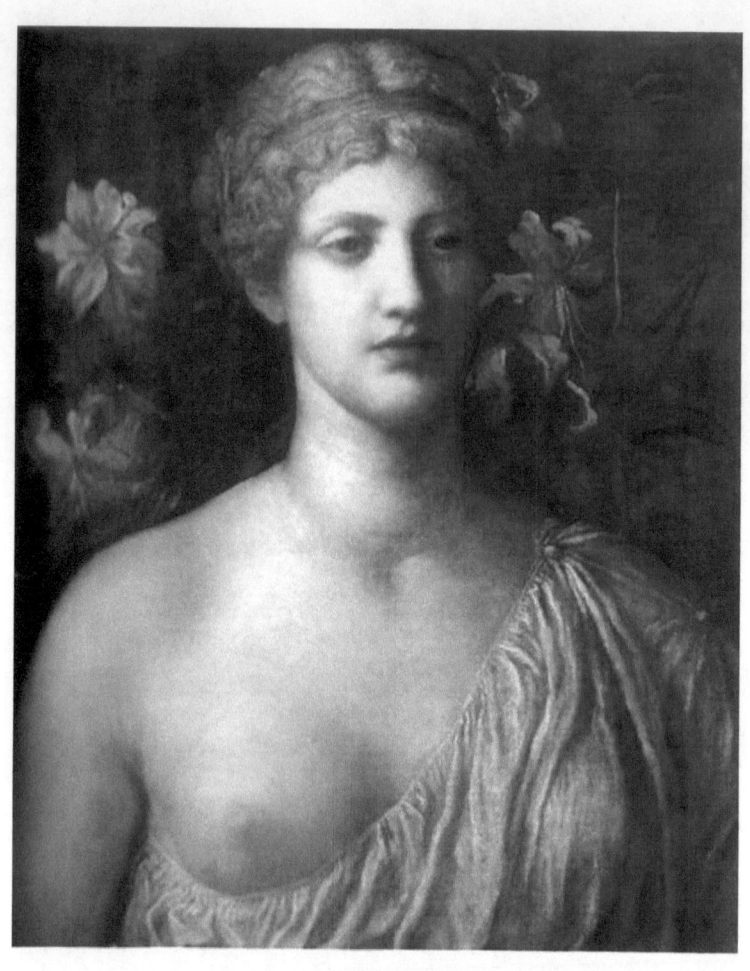

The Wife of Pygmalion, 1868
Oil on canvas

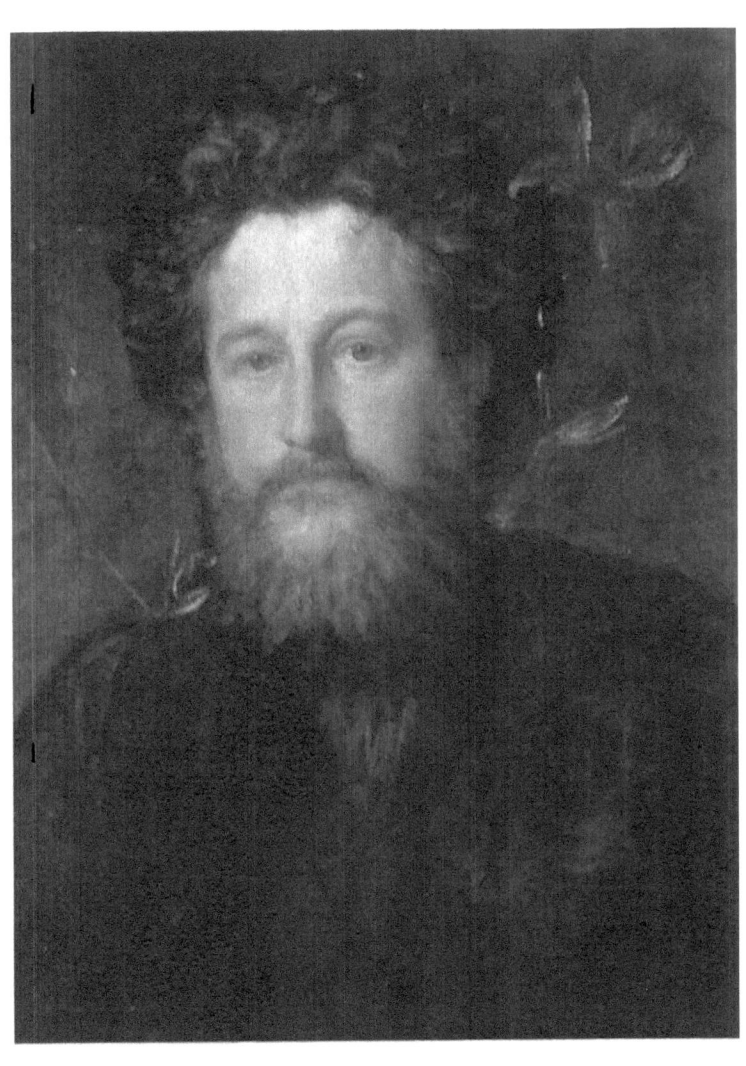

Portrait of William Morris, 1870
Oil on canvas

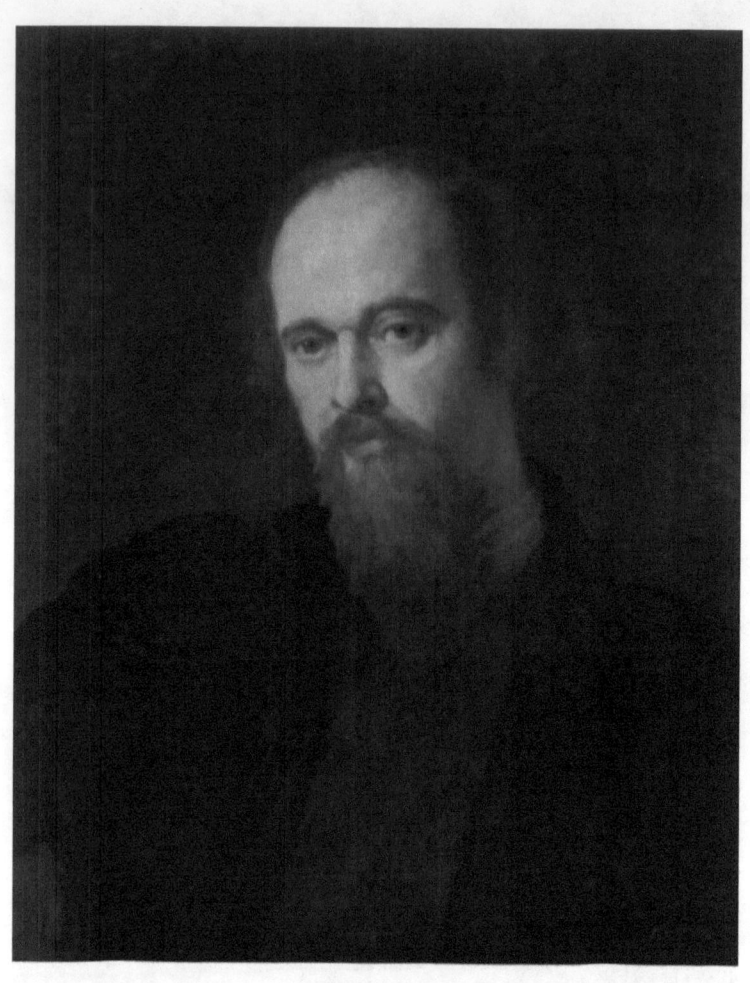

Dante Gabriel Rossetti, 1871
Oil on canvas

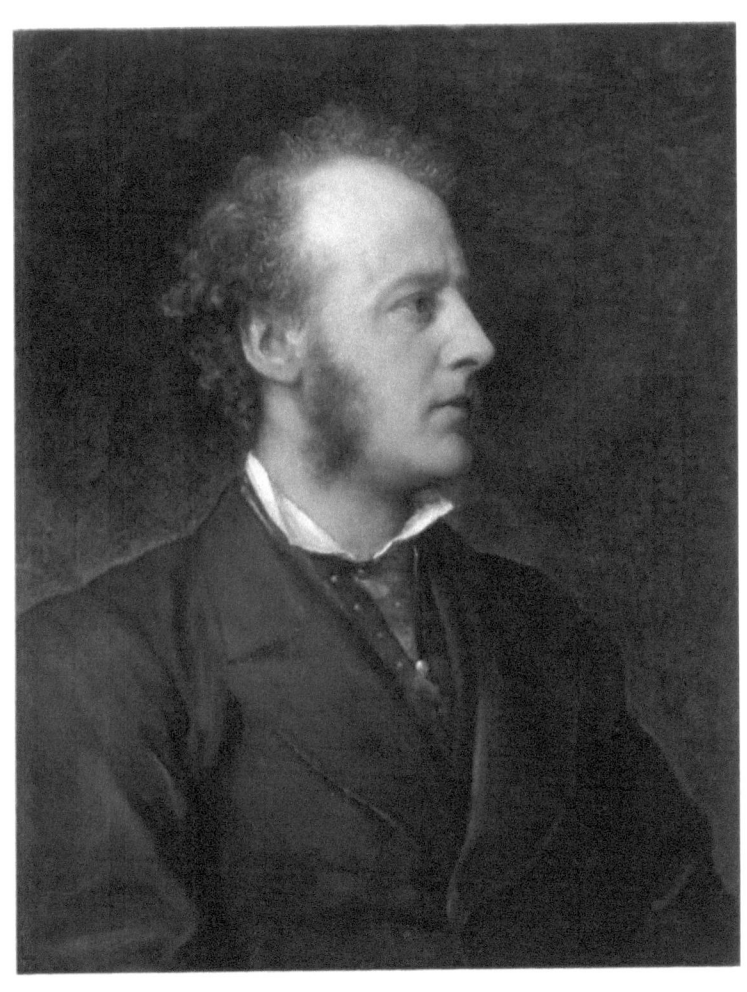

Portrait of Sir John Everett Millais, 1871
Oil on canvas

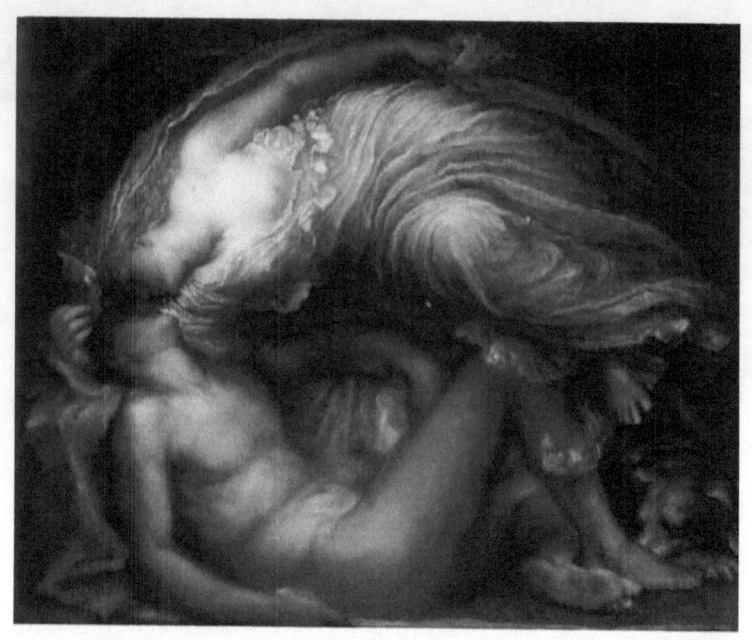

Endymion, 1872
Oil on canvas

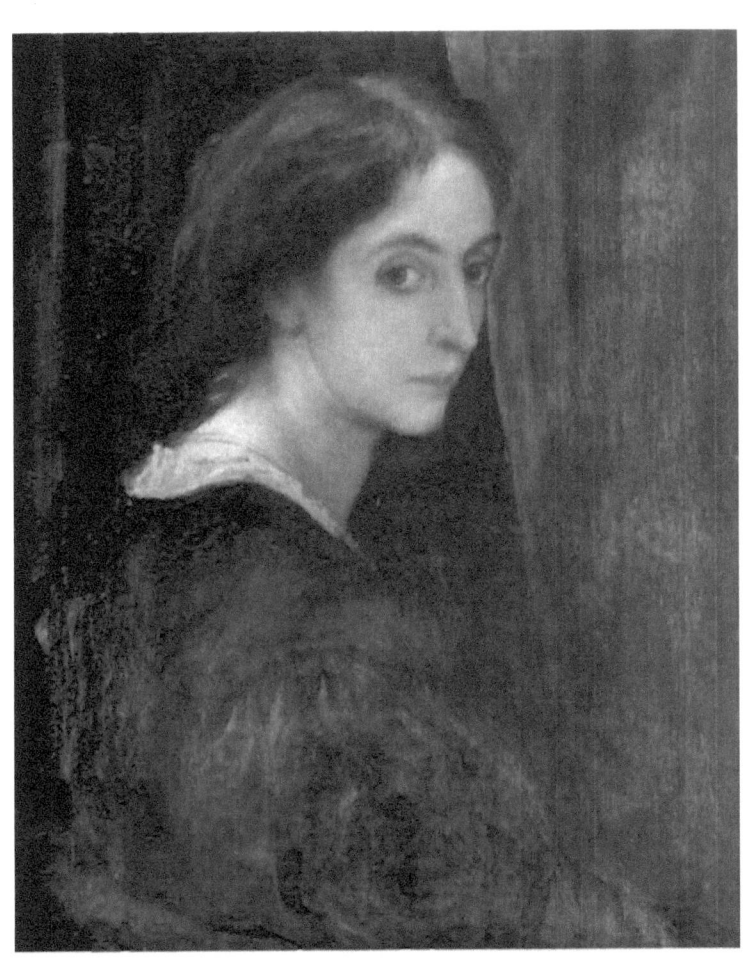

Aglaia Coronio, 1874
Oil on canvas

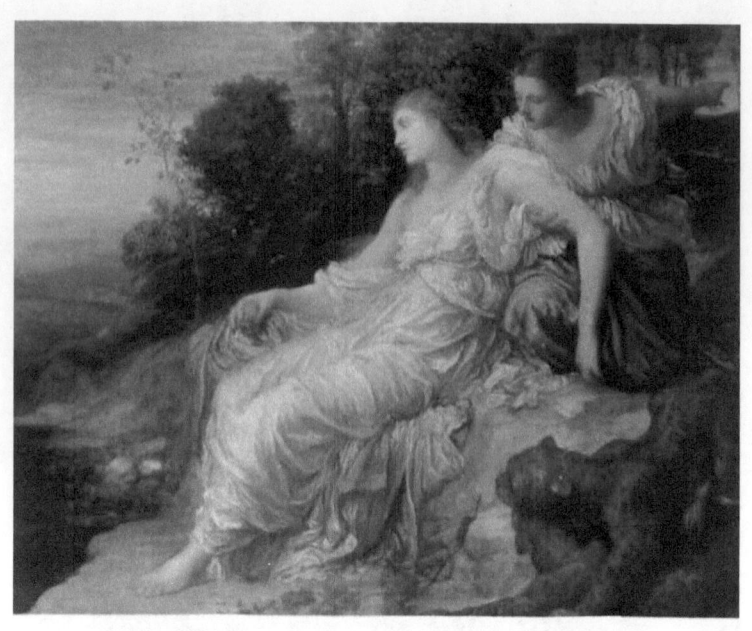

Ariadne on the Island of Naxos, 1875
Oil on canvas

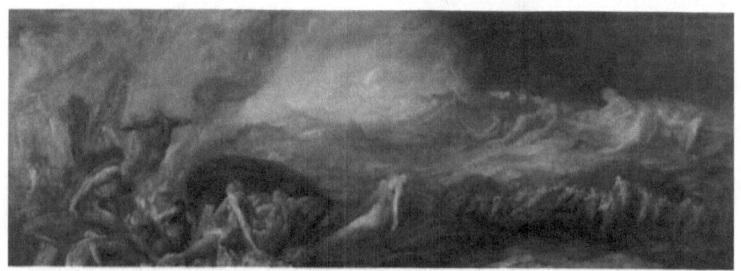

Creation, 1875
Oil on canvas

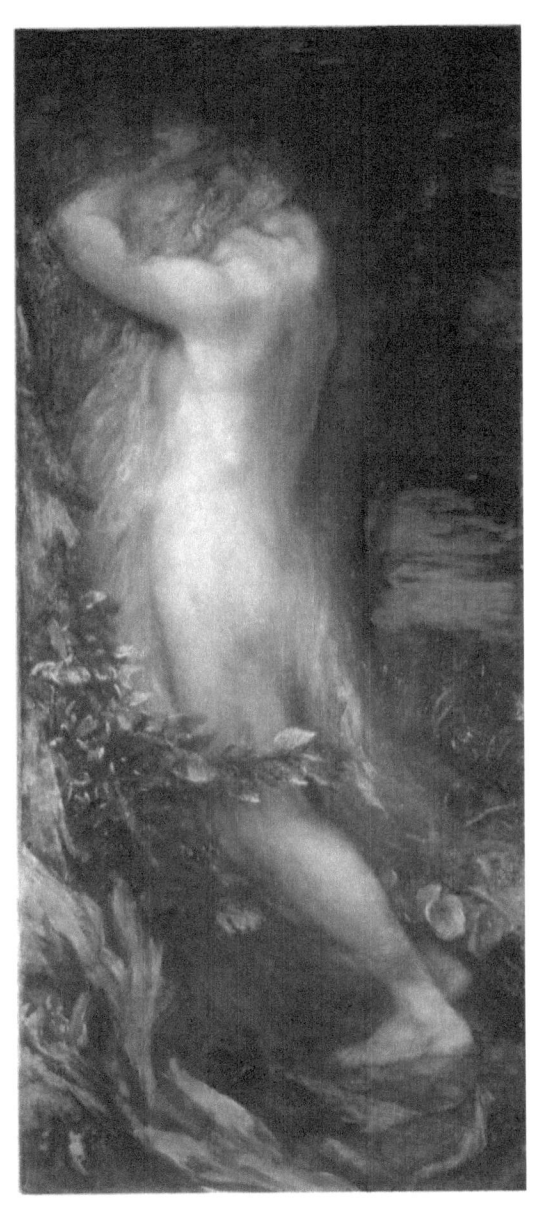

Eve Repentant, 1875
Oil on canvas

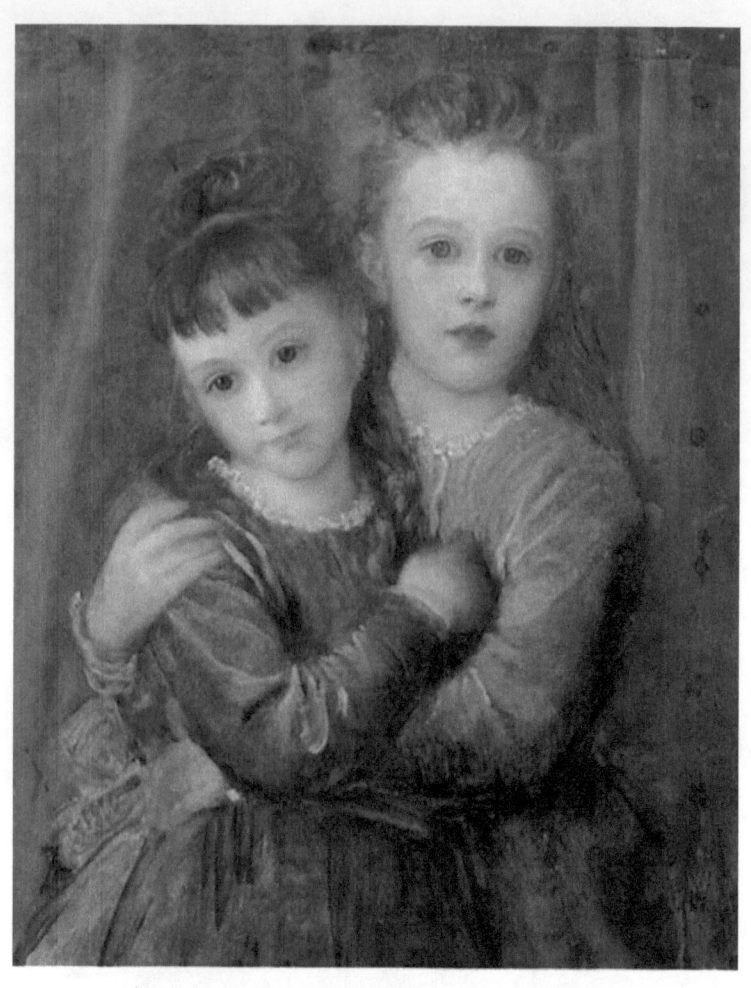

Rachel and Laura Gurney, 1875
Oil on canvas

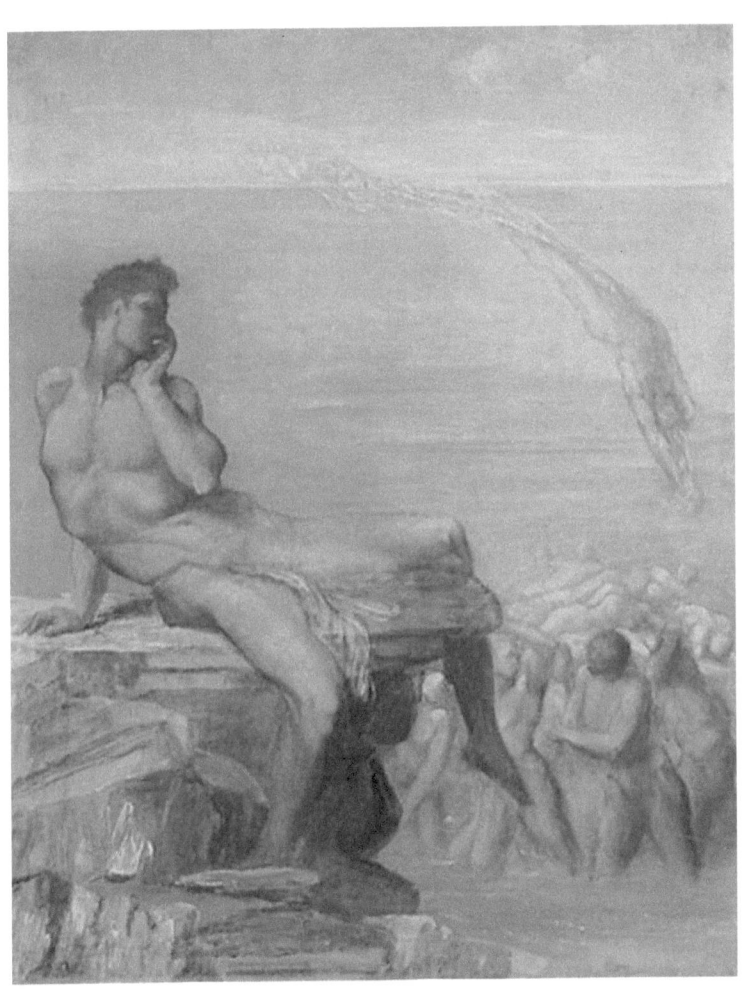

Genius of Greek Poetry, 1878
Oil on canvas

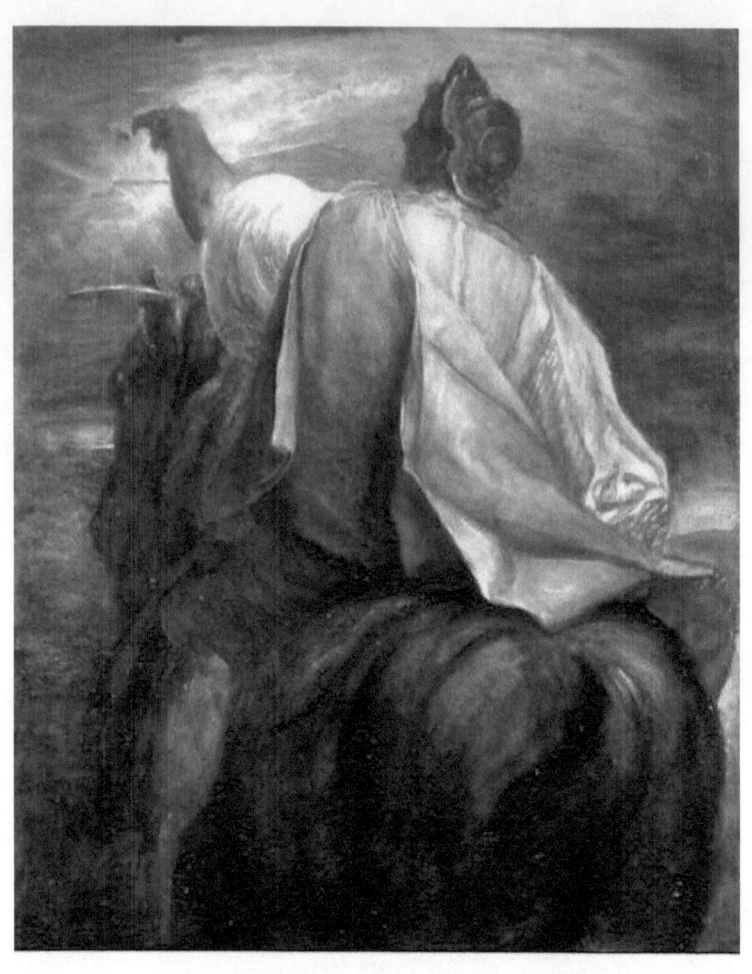

Horsemen apocalypse rider, 1878
Oil on canvas

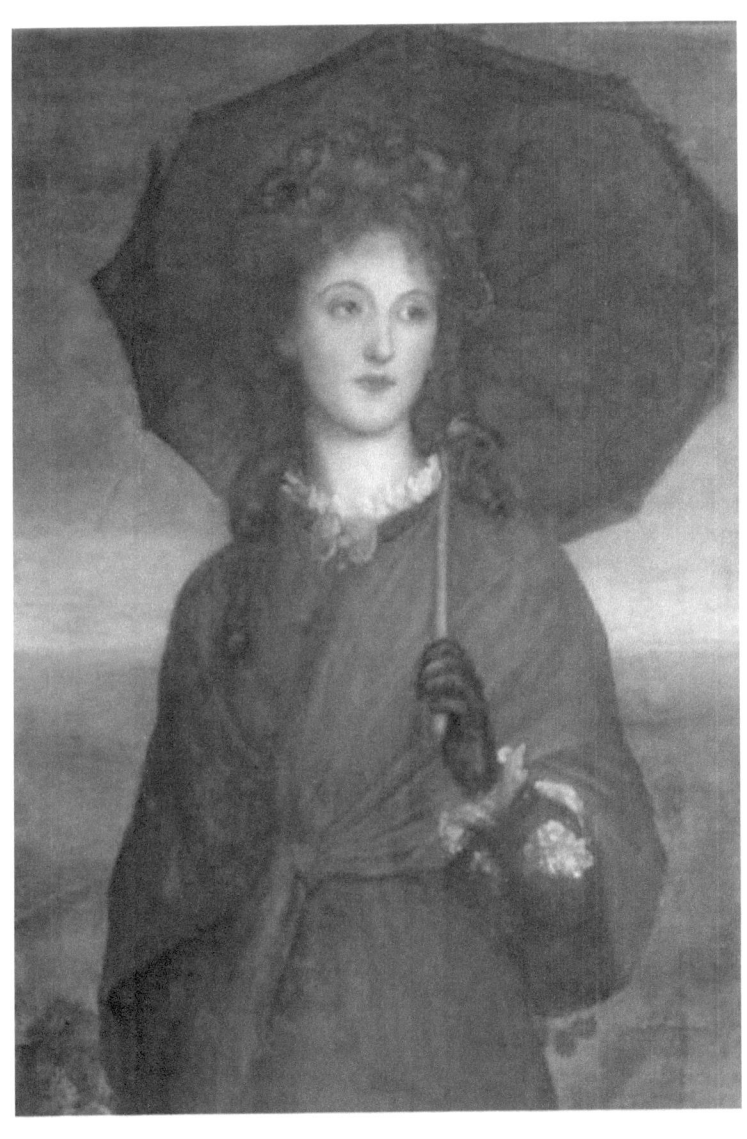

Eveleen Tennant, later Mrs F.W.H. Myers, 1880
Oil on canvas

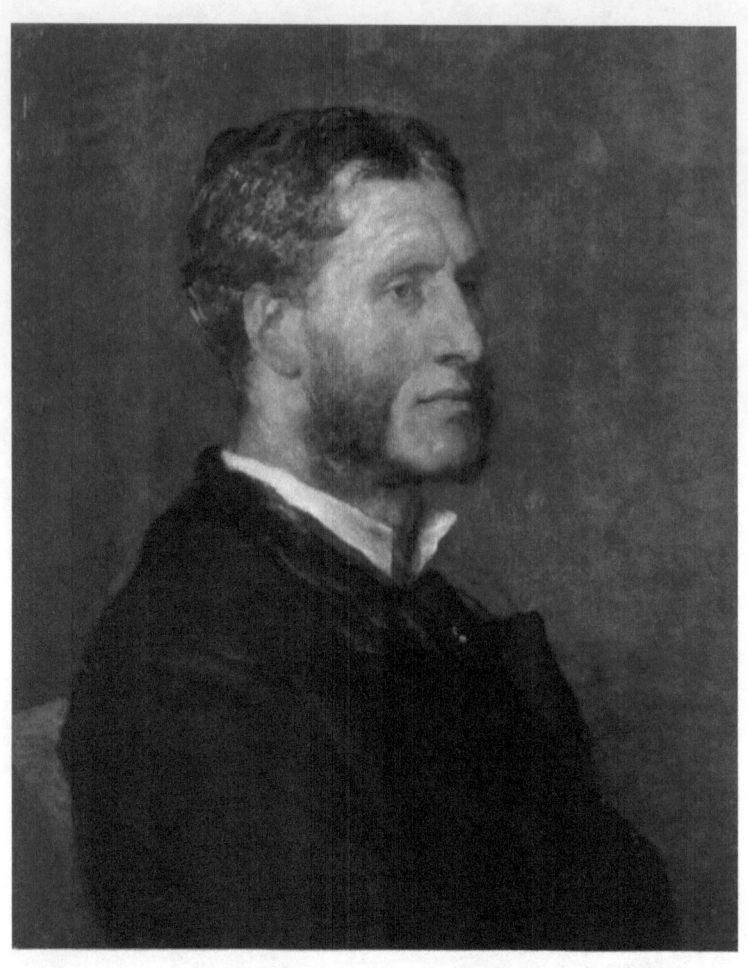

Matthew Arnold, 1880
Oil on canvas

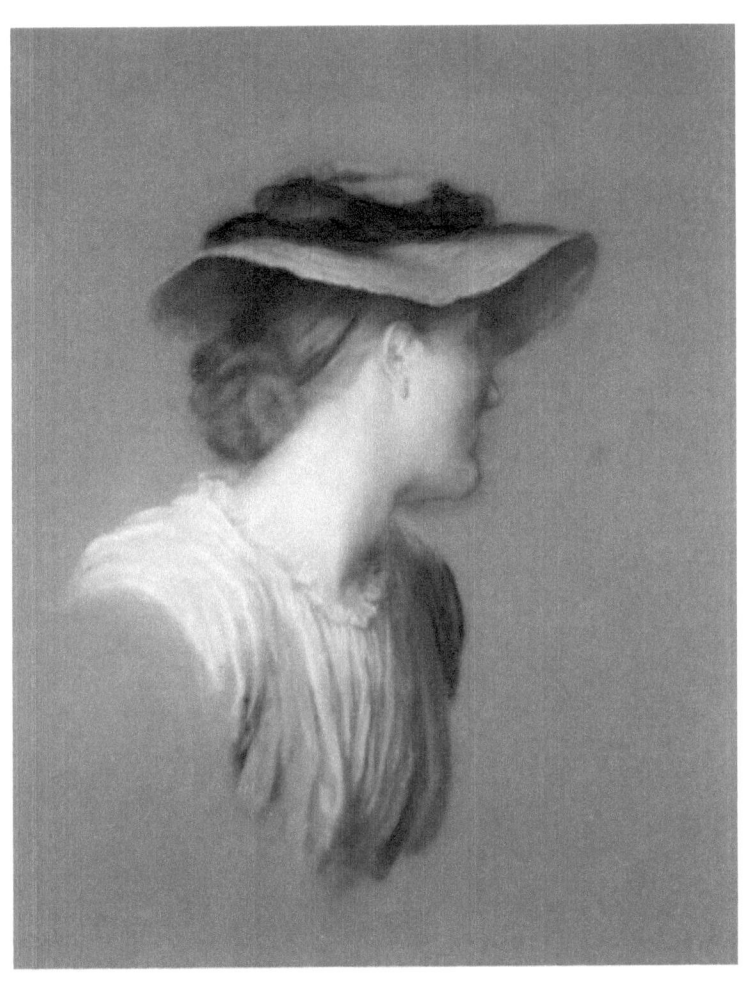

Portrait of the Artist's Wife Mary, c.1880
Oil on board

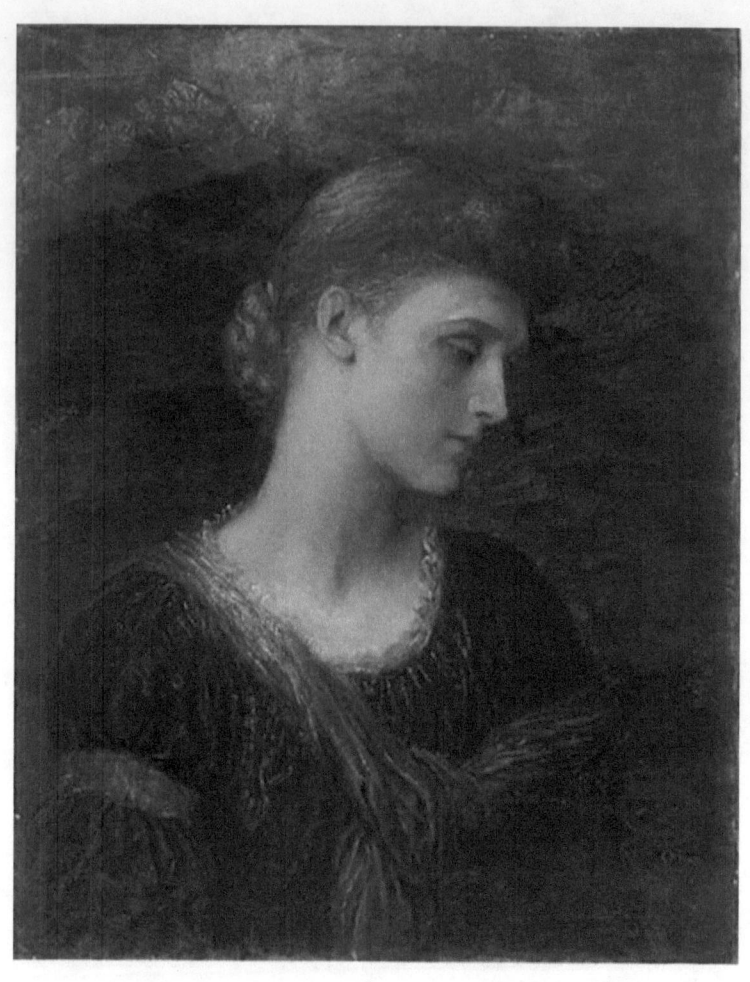

Violet Lindsay, 1881
Oil on canvas

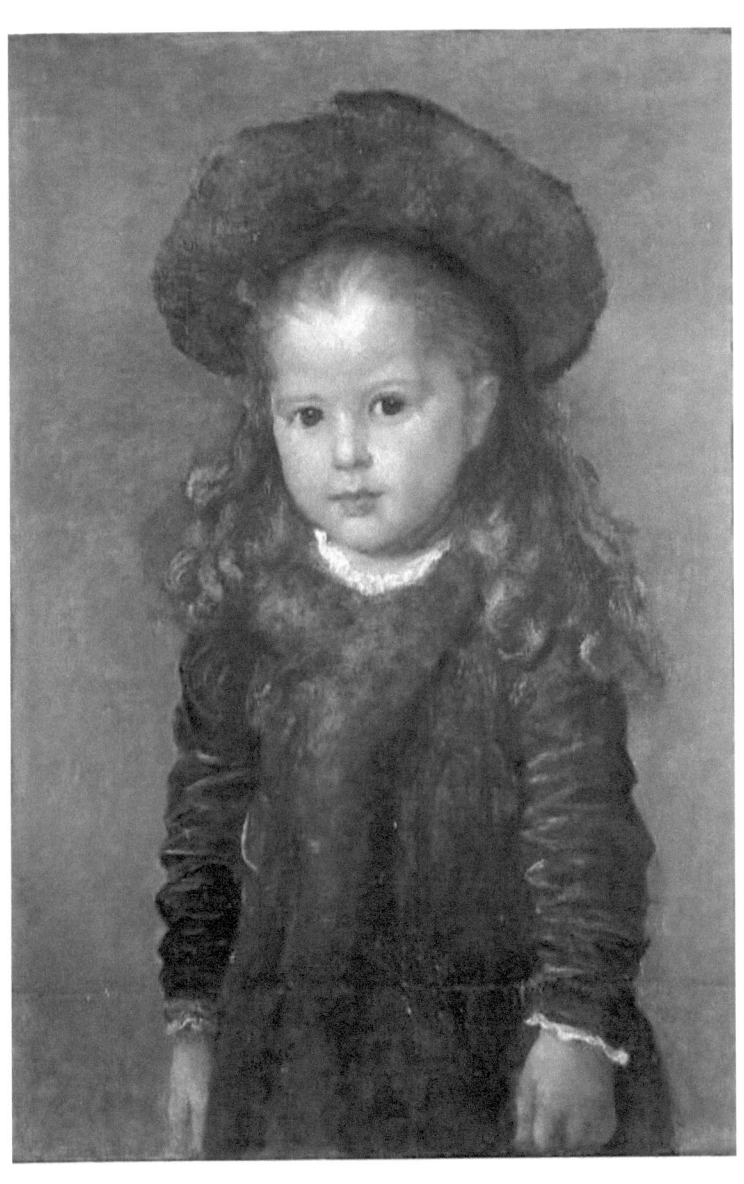

Zoe Ionides, 1881
Oil on canvas

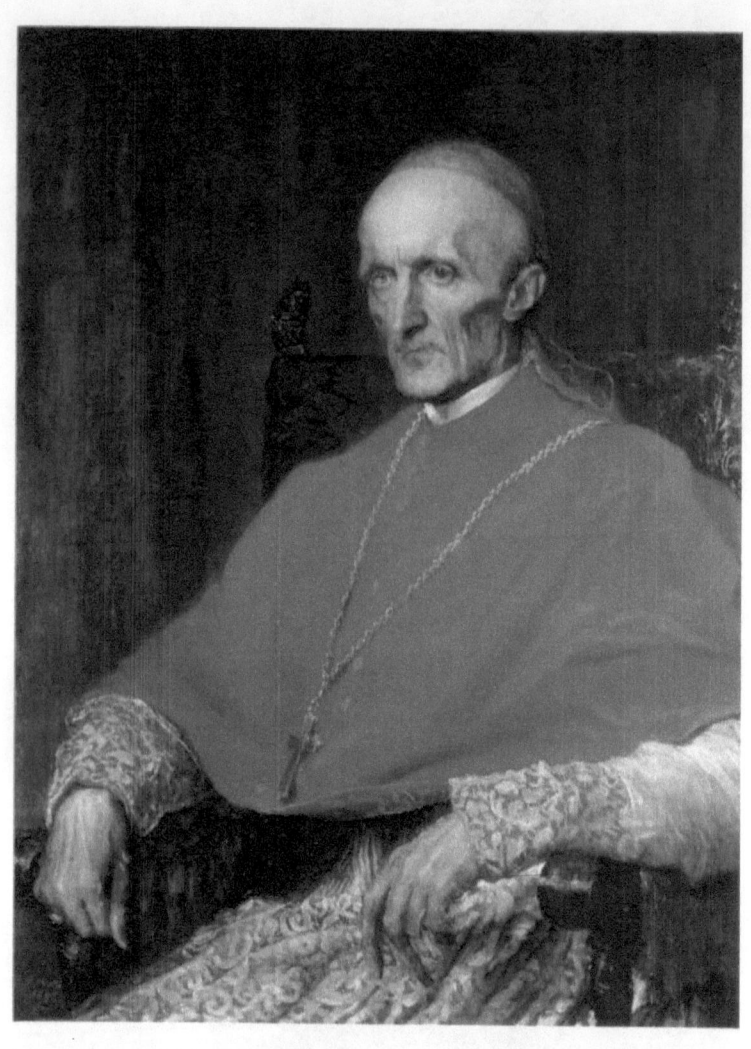

Cardinal Manning, 1882
Oil on canvas

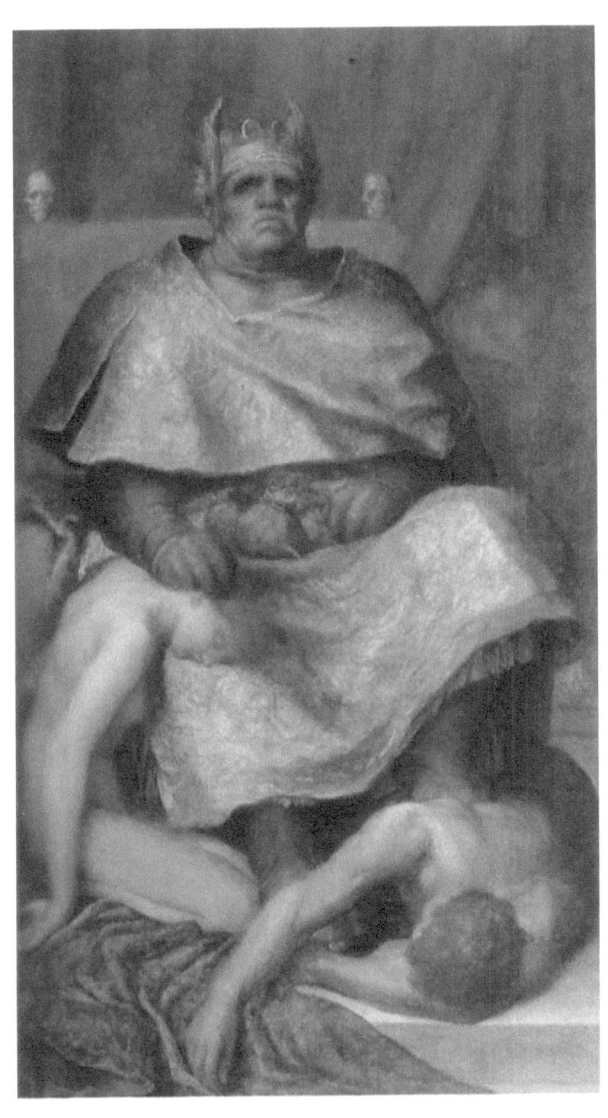

Mammon, 1884-1885
Oil on canvas

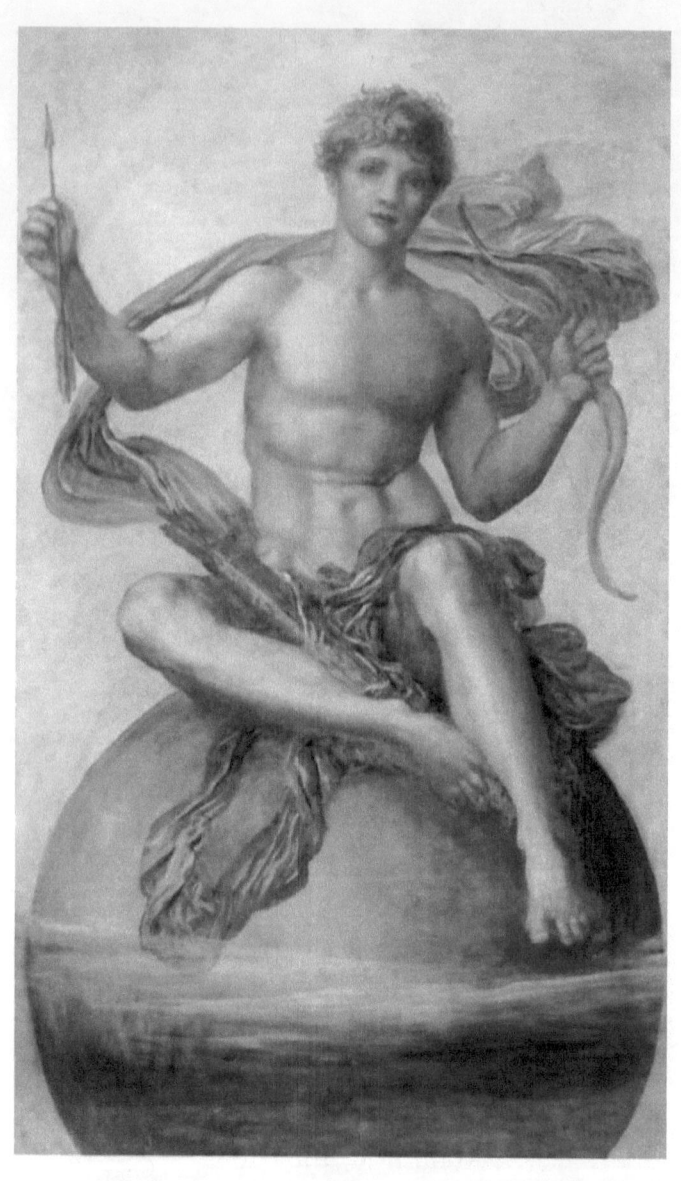

Study of Idle Child of Fancy, c.1885
Oil on canvas

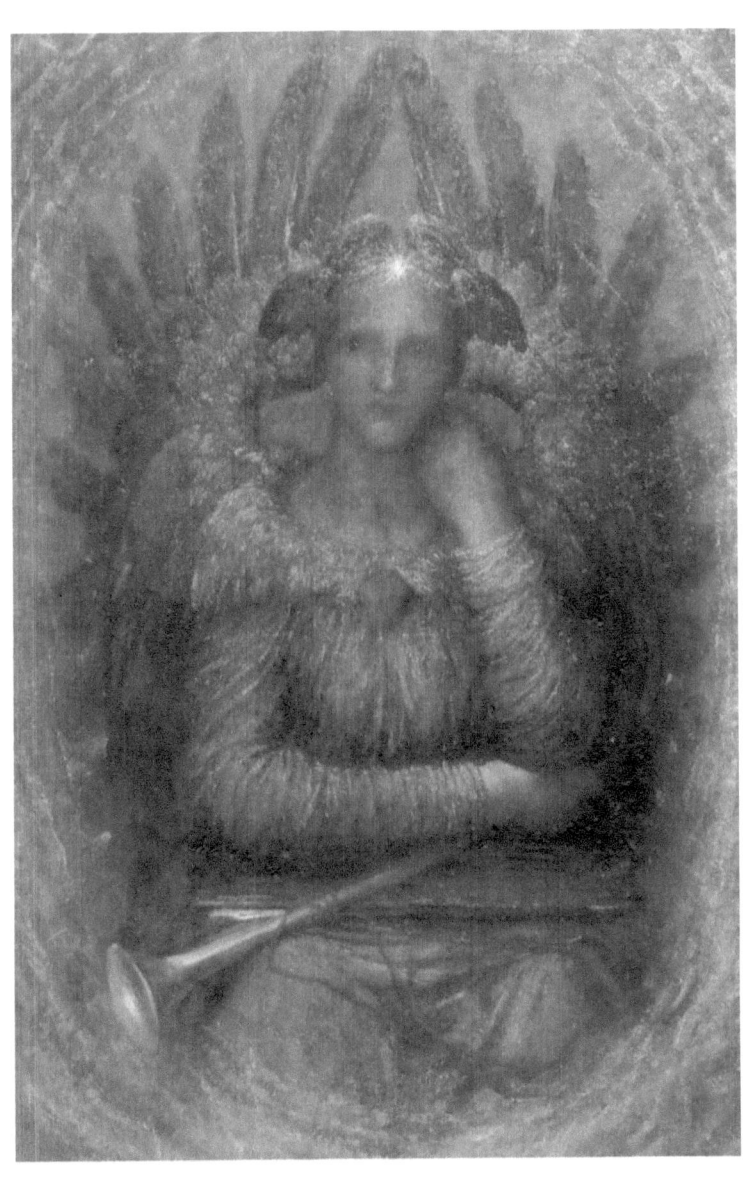

Dweller Within, 1885-1886
Oil on canvas

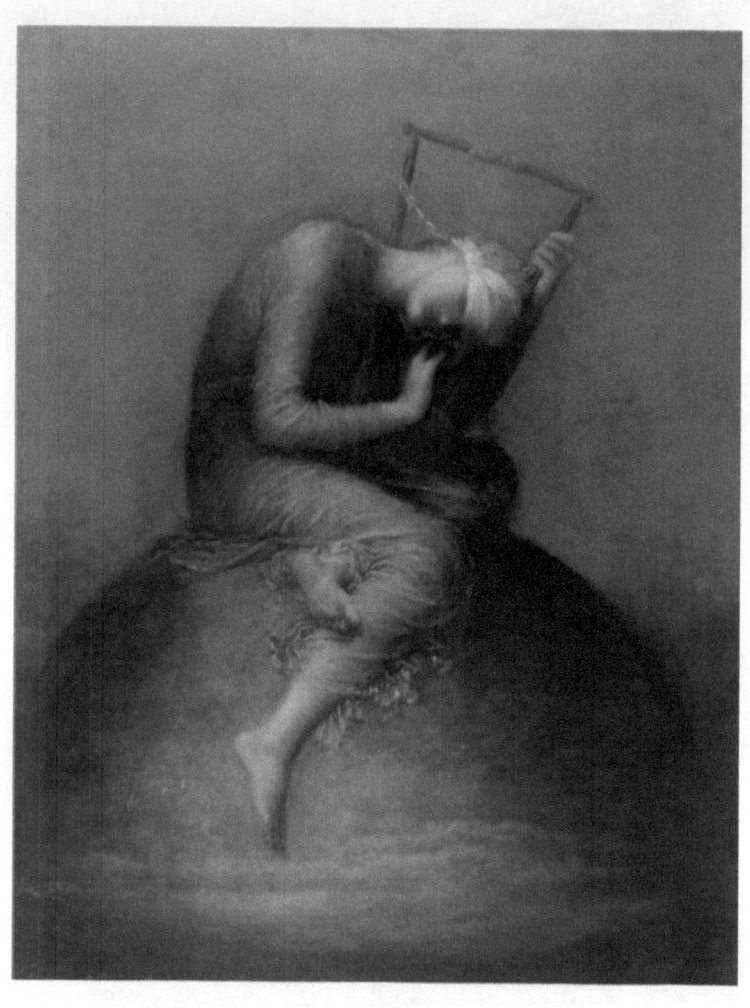

Hope, 1886
Oil on canvas

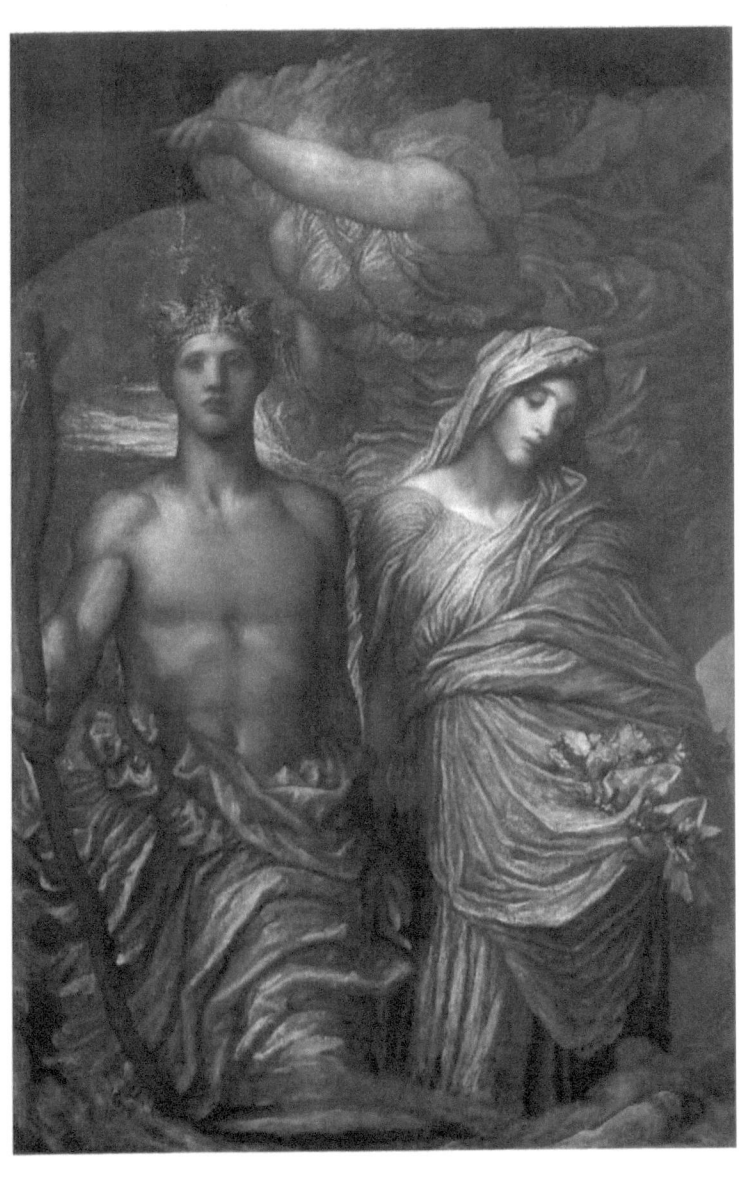

Time, Death and Judgement, 1870-1886
Oil on canvas

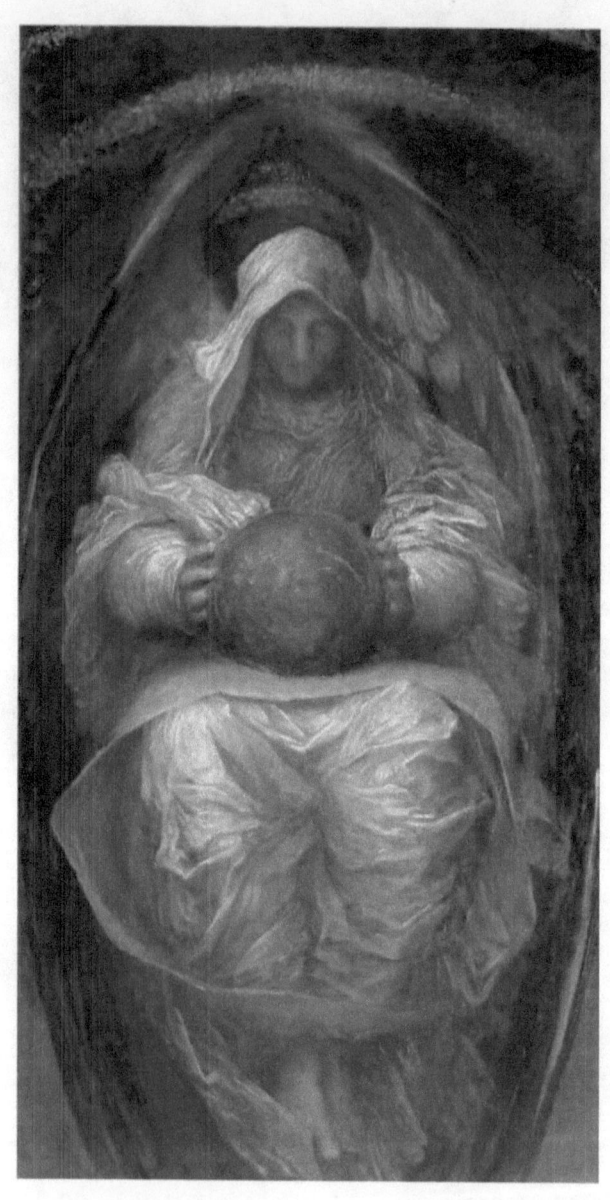

All Pervading, c.1887
Oil on canvas

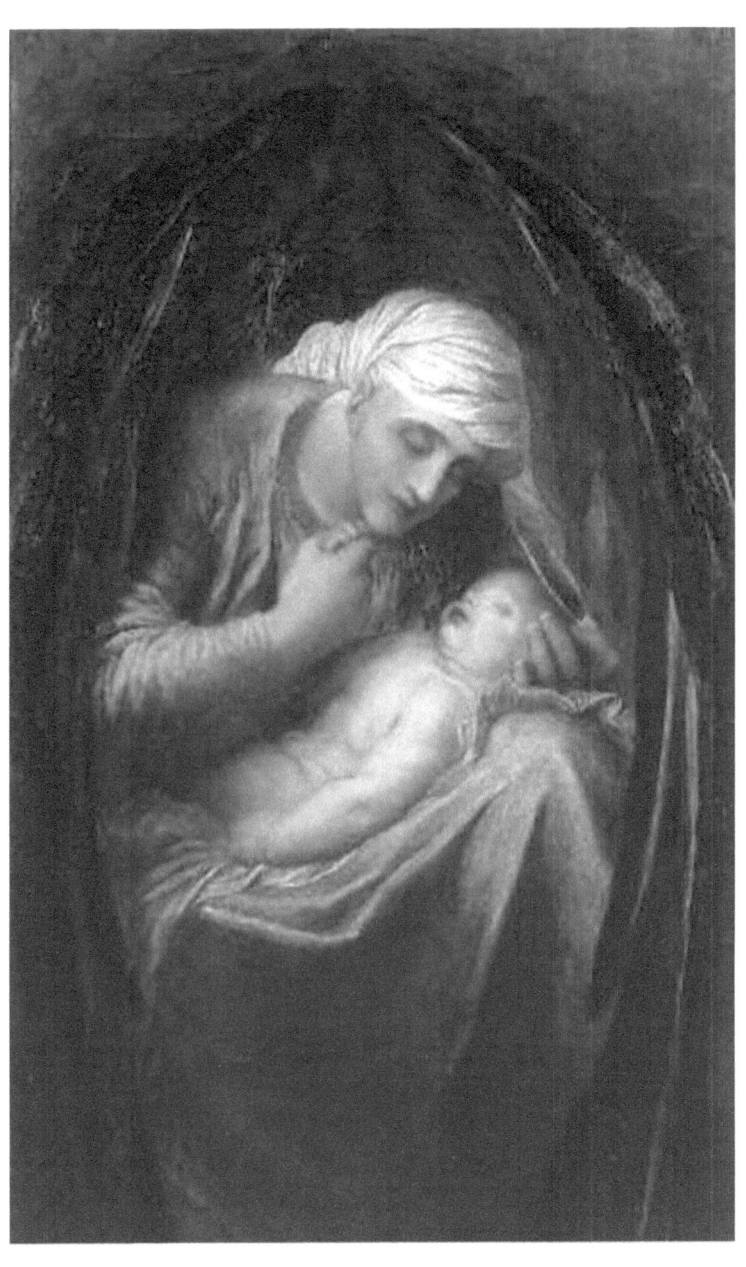

Death Crowning Innocence, 1886-1887
Oil on canvas

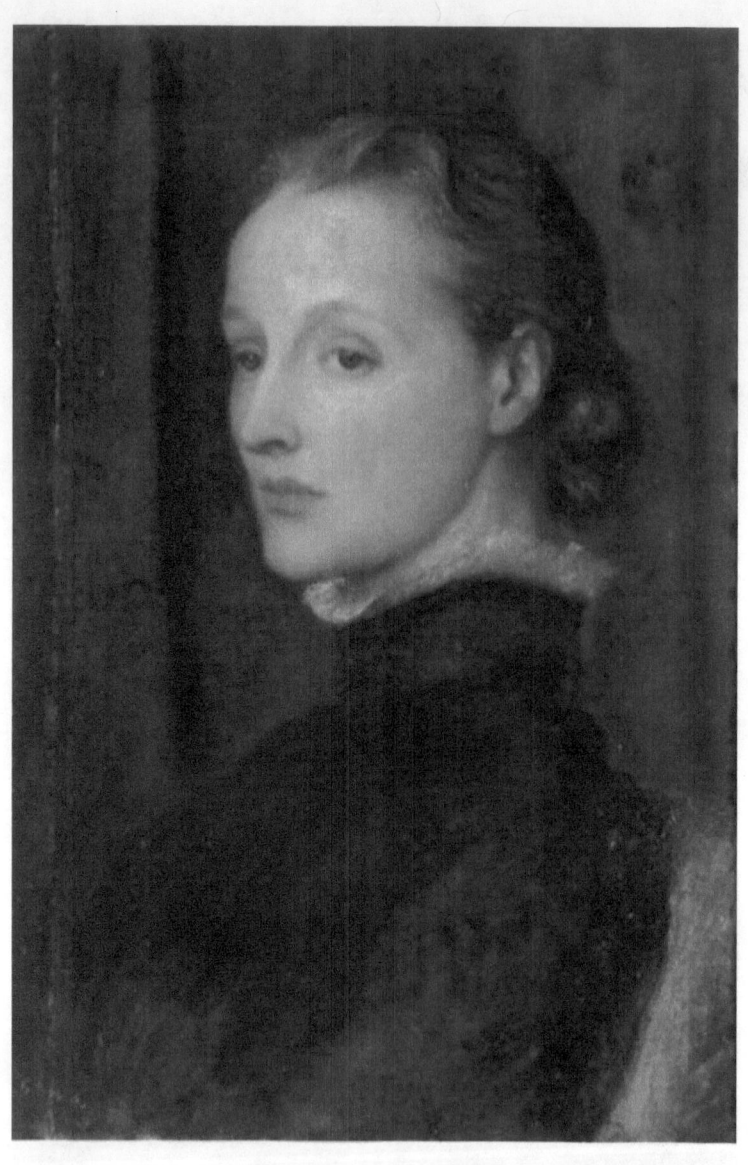

Portrait of Mary Fraser Tytler, afterwards Mary Seton
Watts, 1887
Oil on canvas

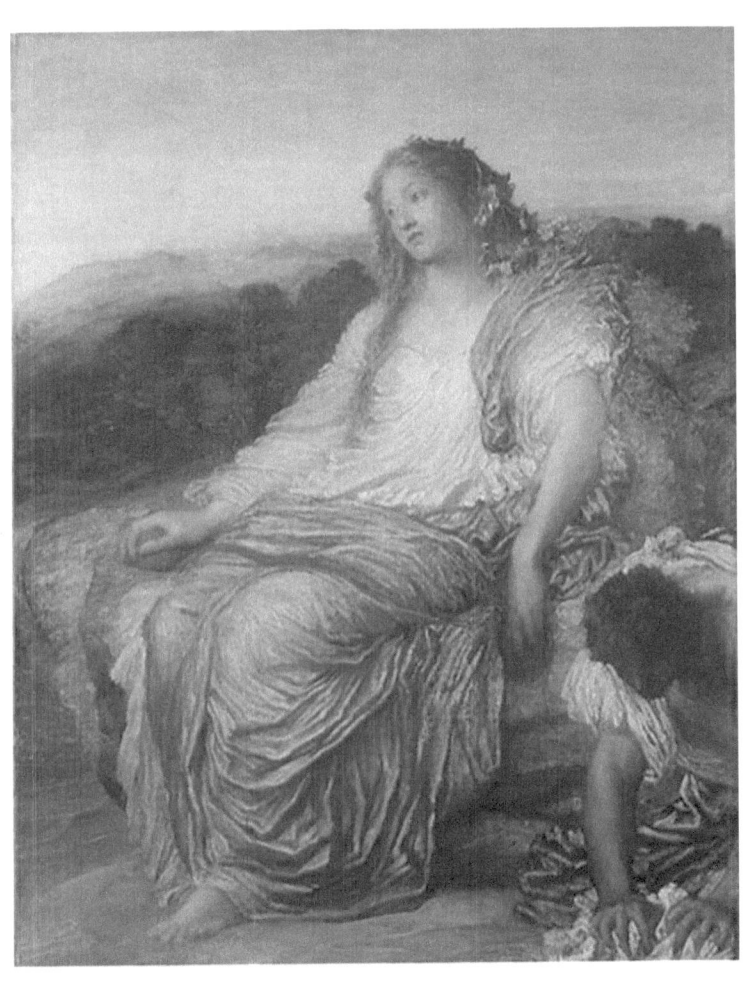

Ariadne, 1890
Oil on canvas

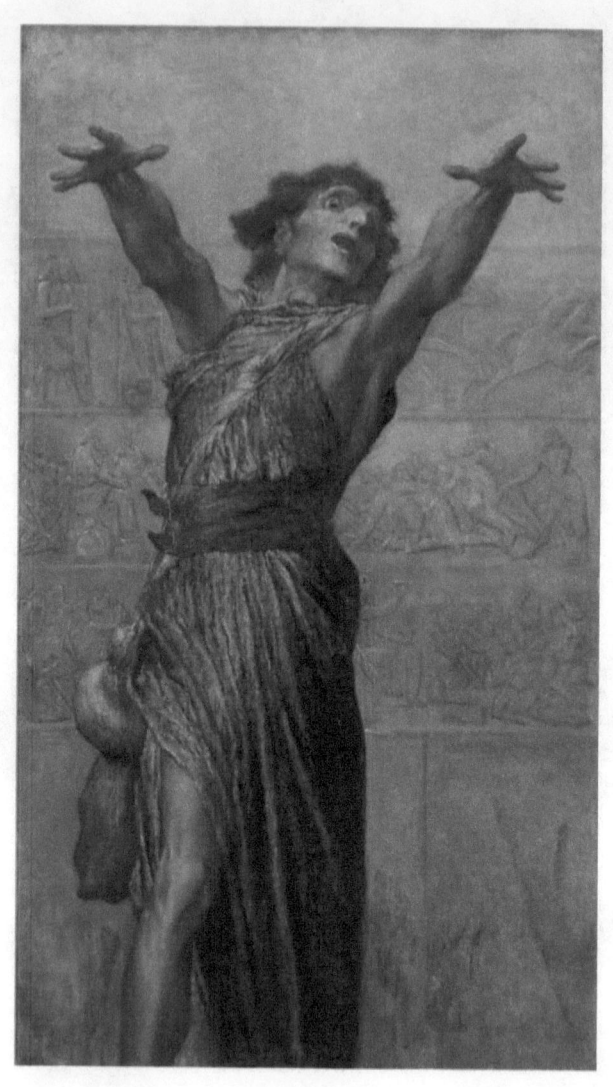

Jonah, 1894
Oil on canvas

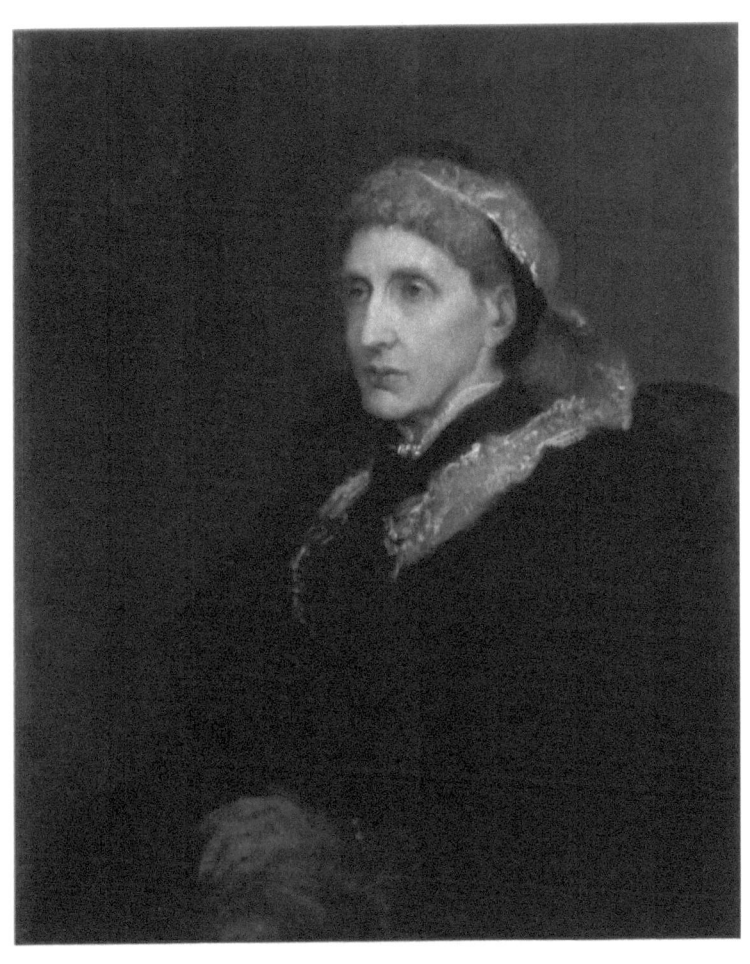

Josephine Elizabeth Butler (née Grey), 1894
Oil on canvas

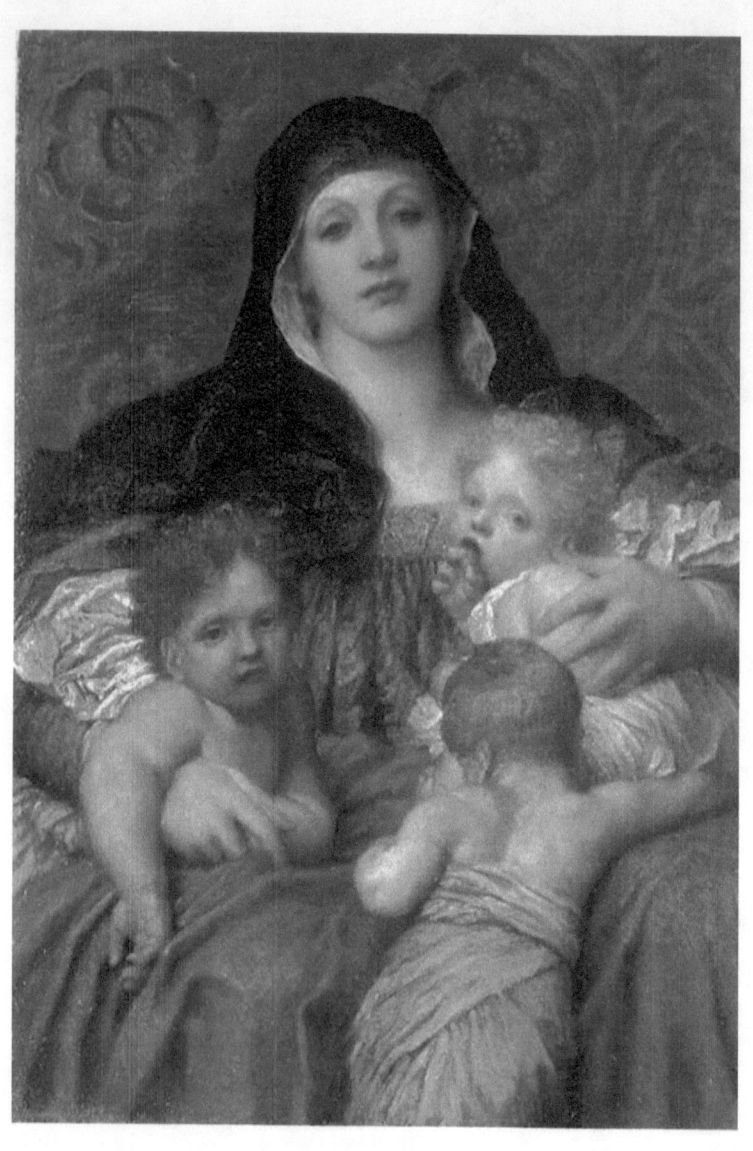

Charity, 1898
Oil on canvas

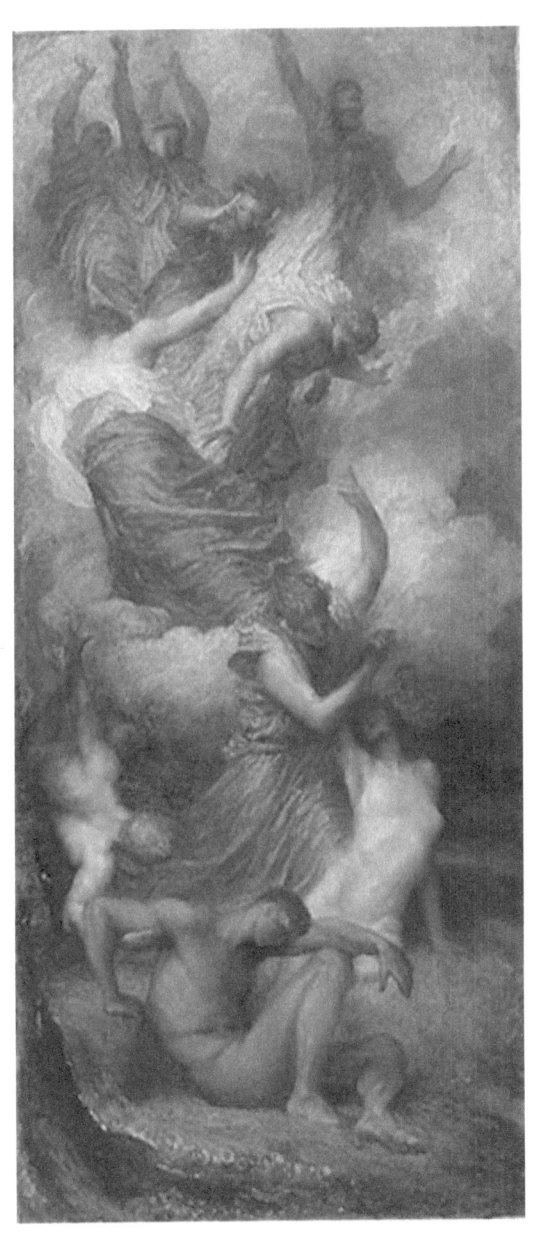

Creation of Eve, c.1865-c.1899
Oil on canvas

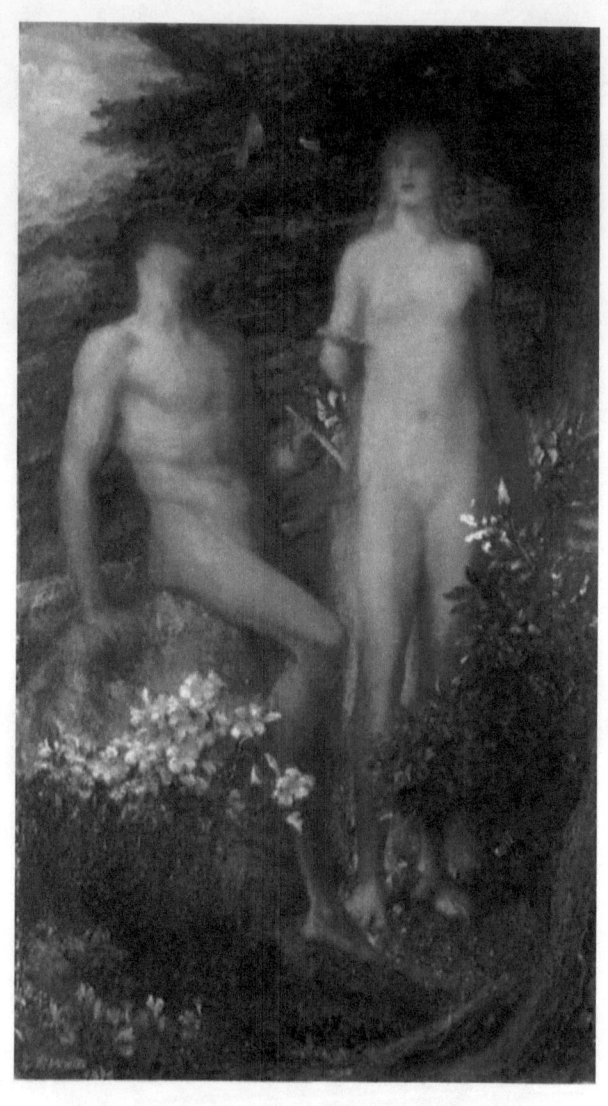

Adam and Eve before the Temptation
Oil on canvas

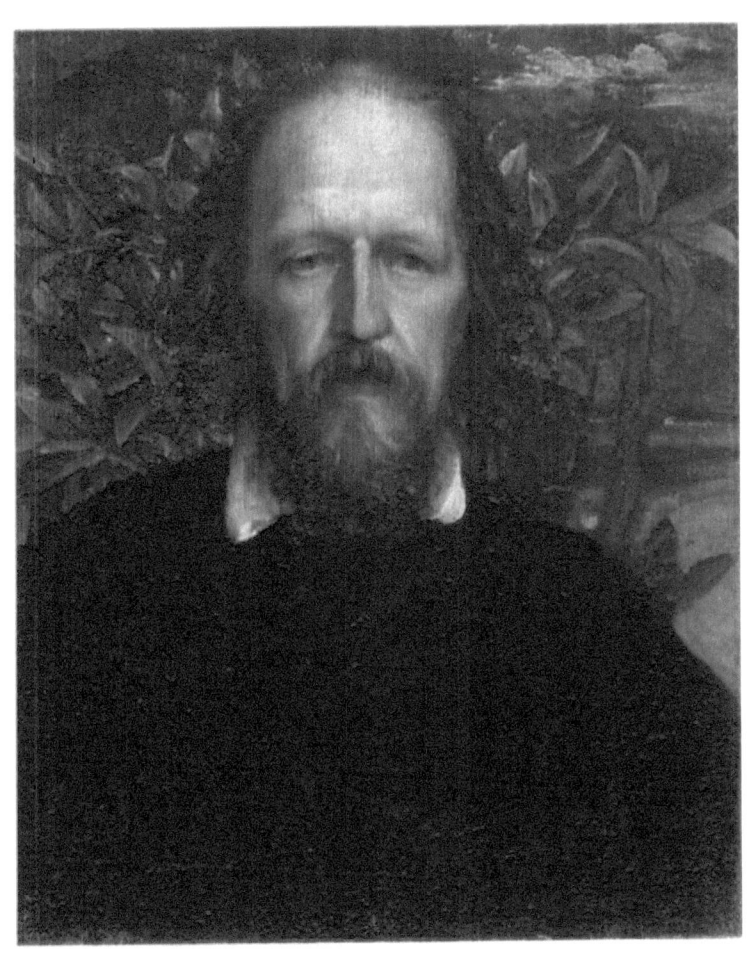

Alfred Tennyson, 1st Baron Tennyson
Oil on canvas

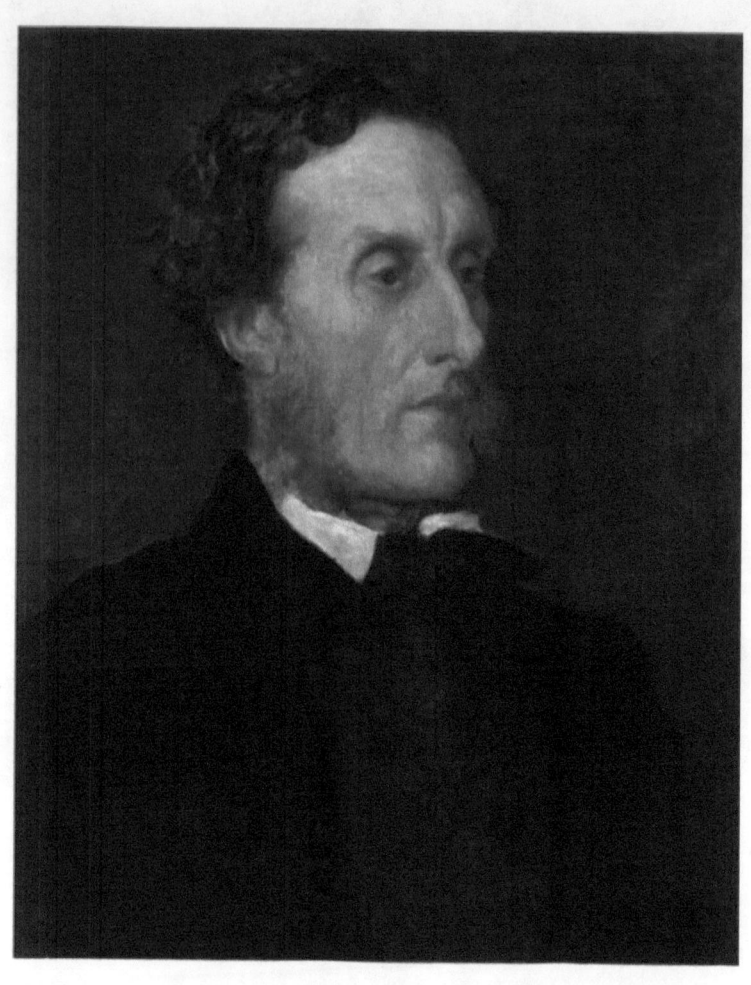

Anthony Ashley Cooper, 7th Earl of Shaftesbury
Oil on canvas

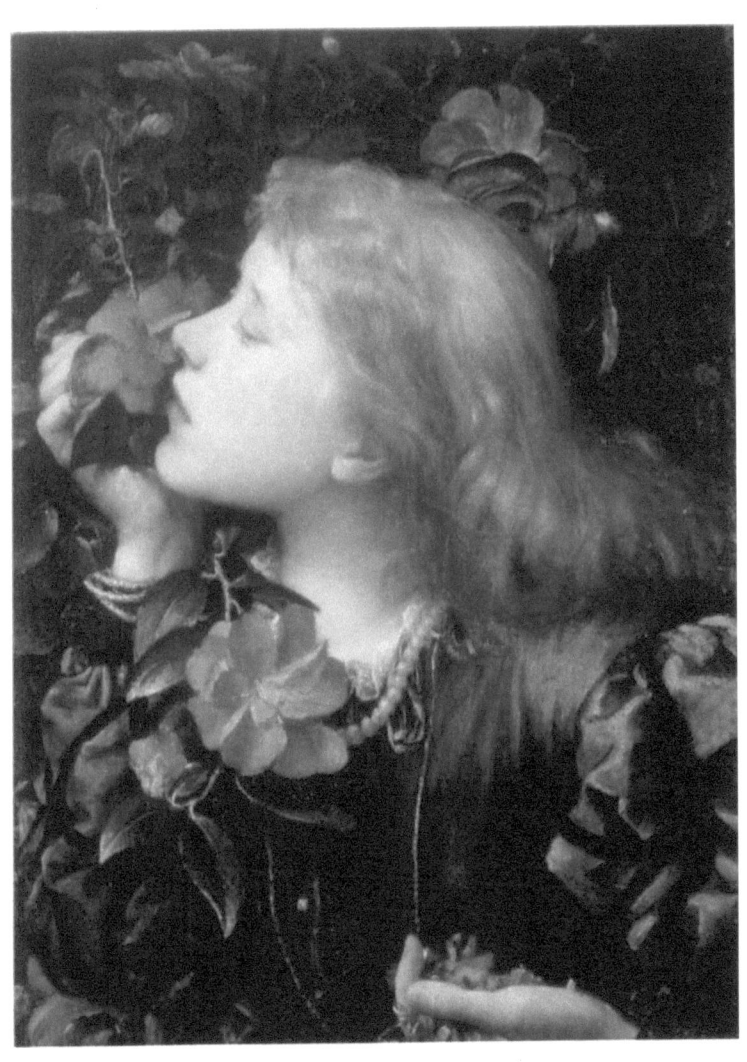

Choosing
Oil on canvas

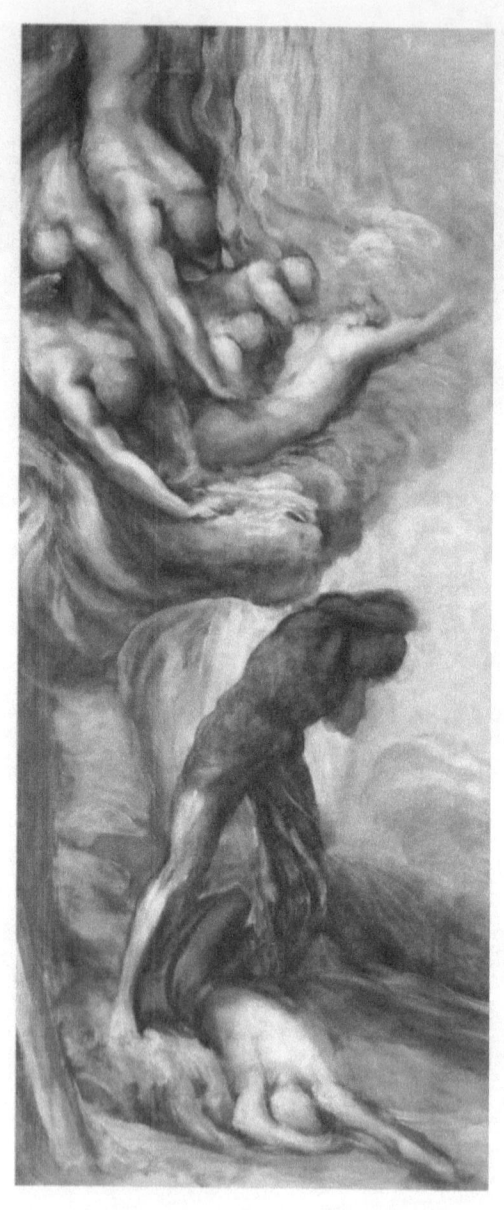

Denunciation of Cain
Oil on canvas

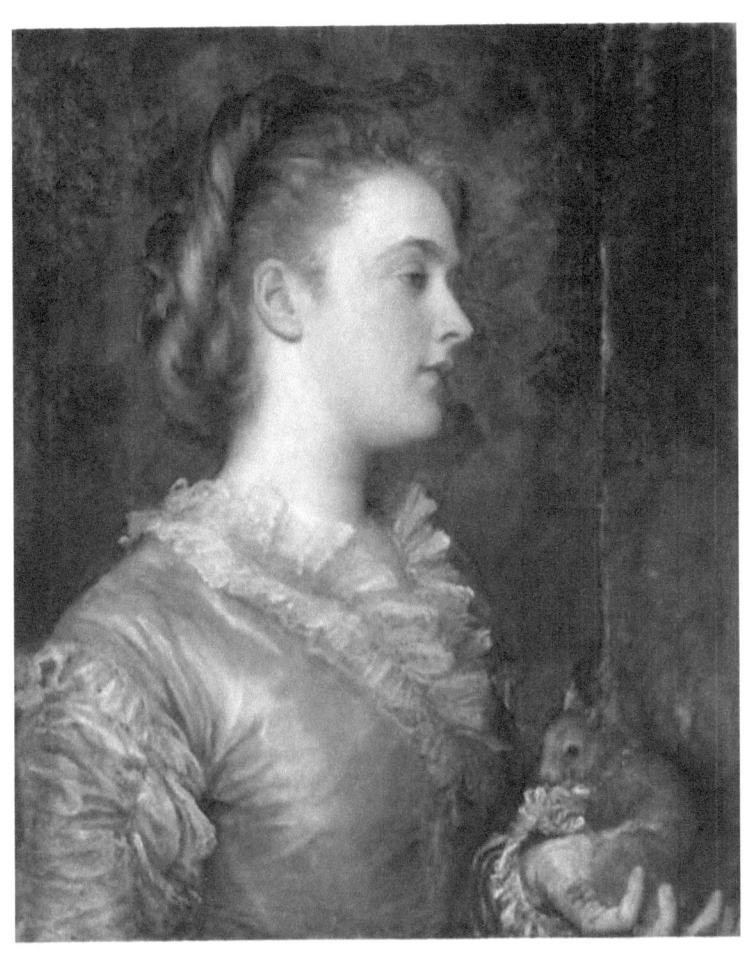

Dorothy Tennant, Later Lady Stanley
Oil on canvas

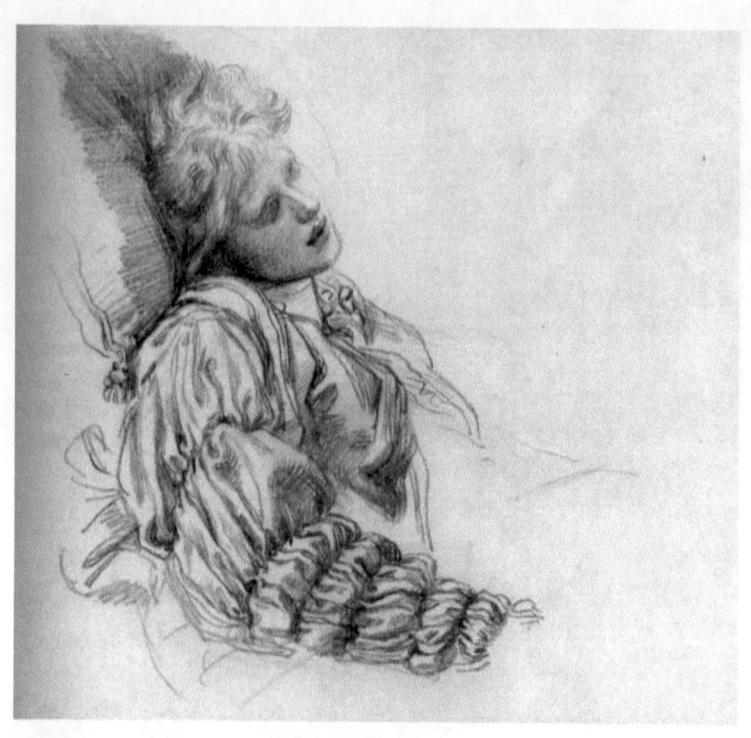

Ellen Terry Asleep
Drawing

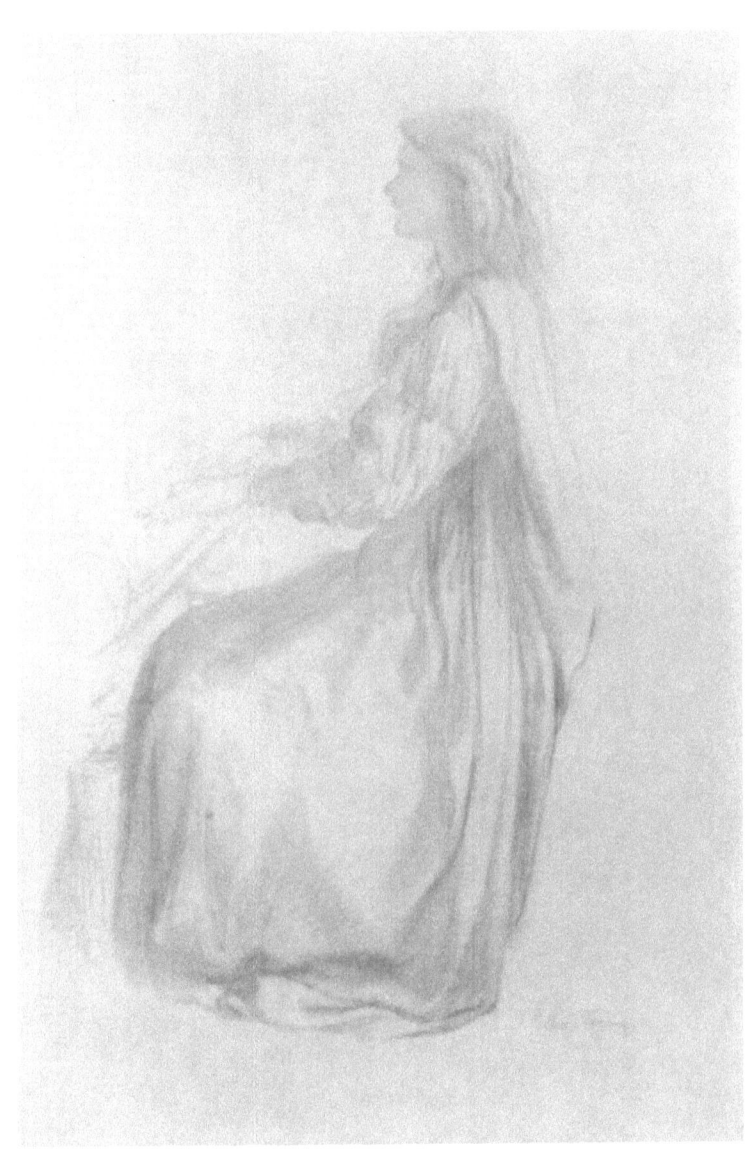

Ellen Terry at the Piano
Drawing

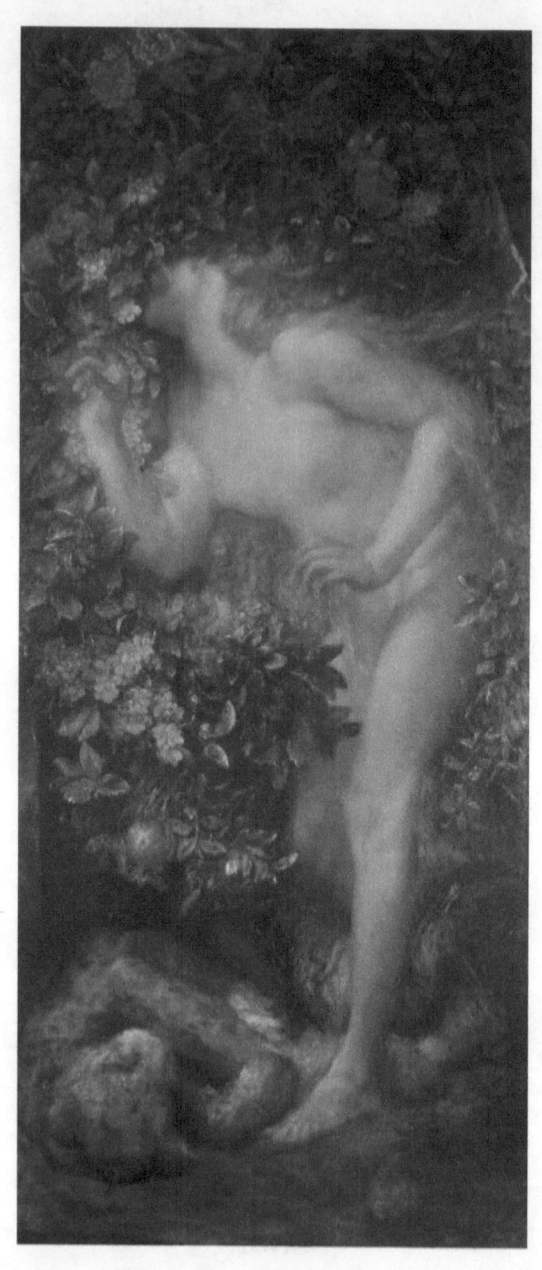

Eve Tempted
Oil on canvas

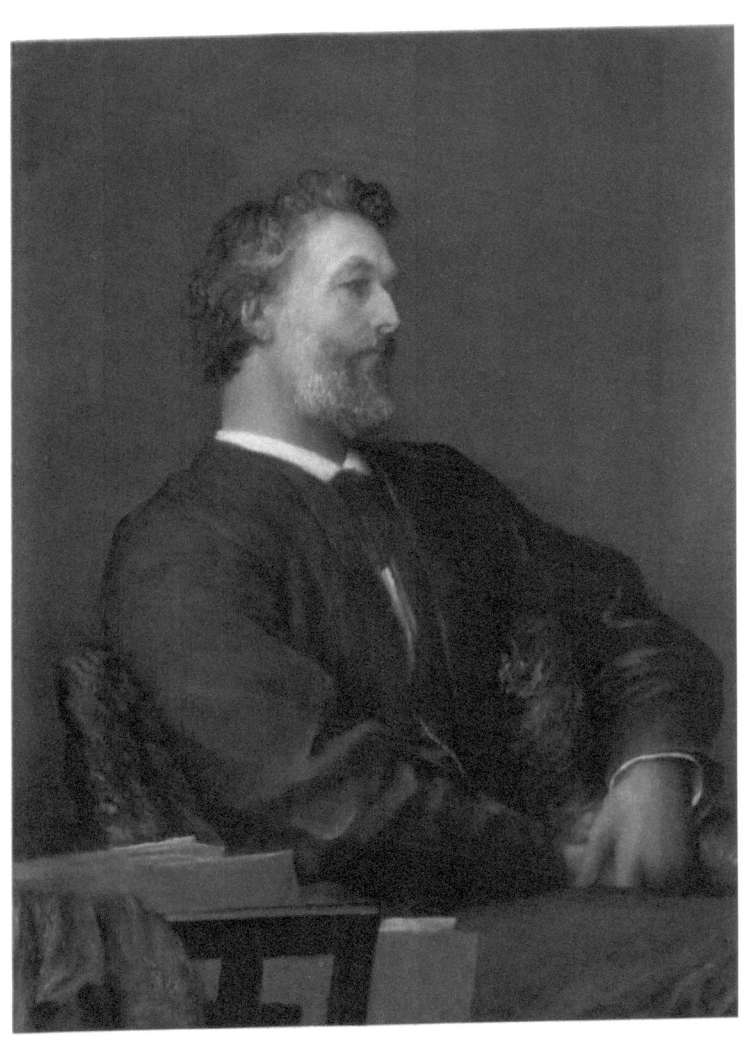

Frederic Leighton, Baron Leighton
Oil on canvas

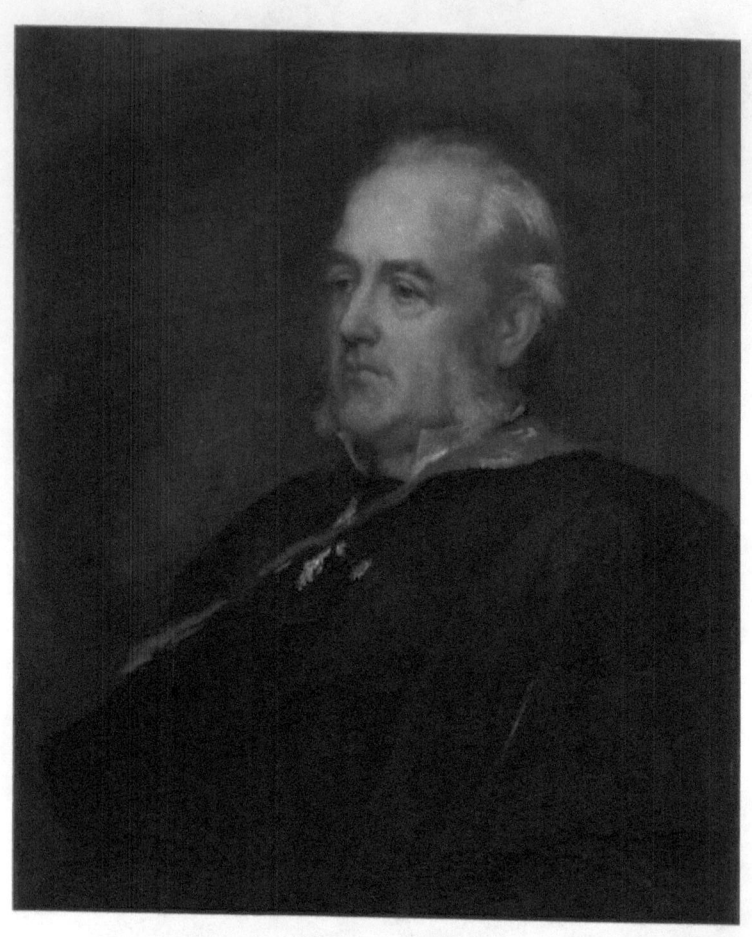

Friedrich Max Müller
Oil on canvas

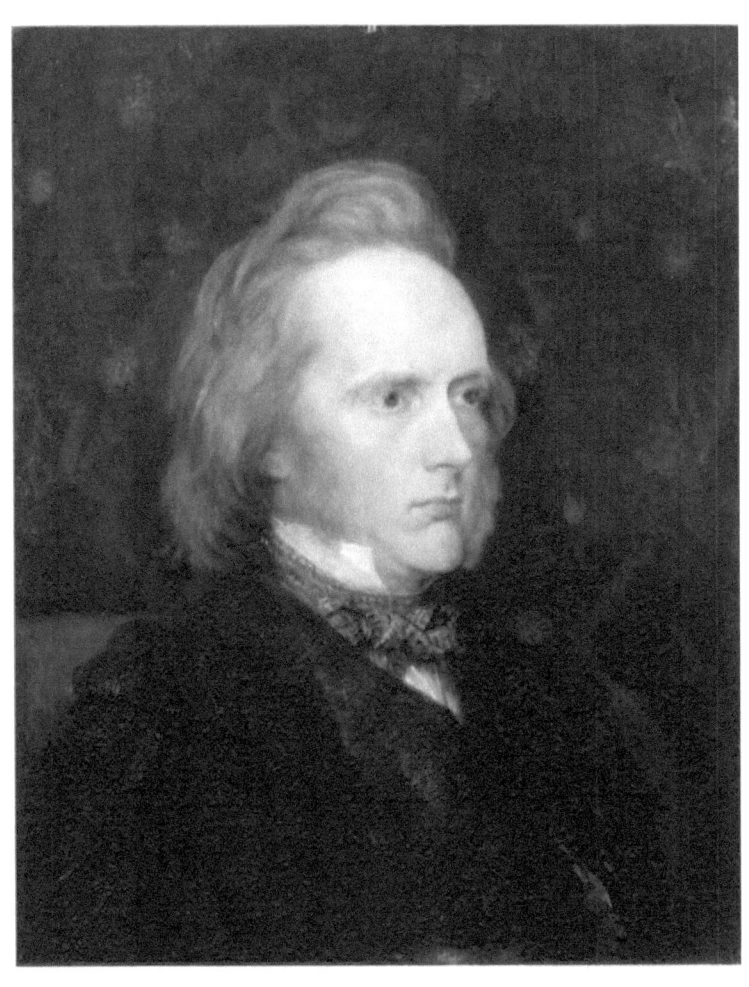

George Douglas Campbell, 8th Duke of Argyll
Oil on canvas

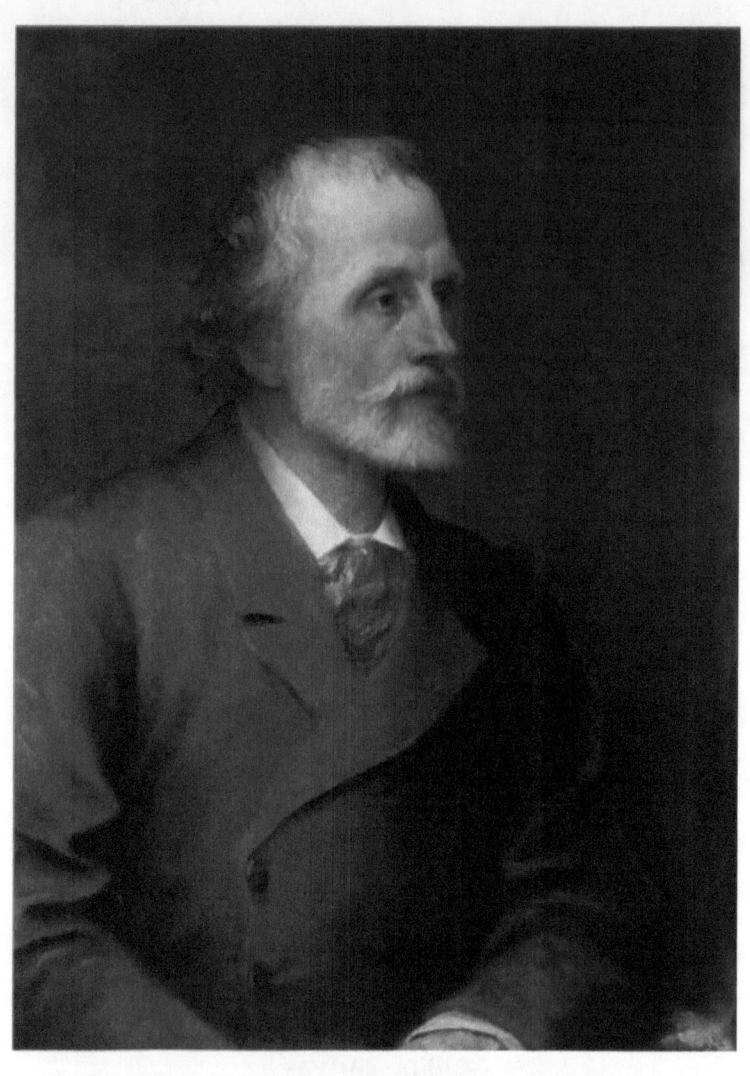

George Meredith
Oil on canvas

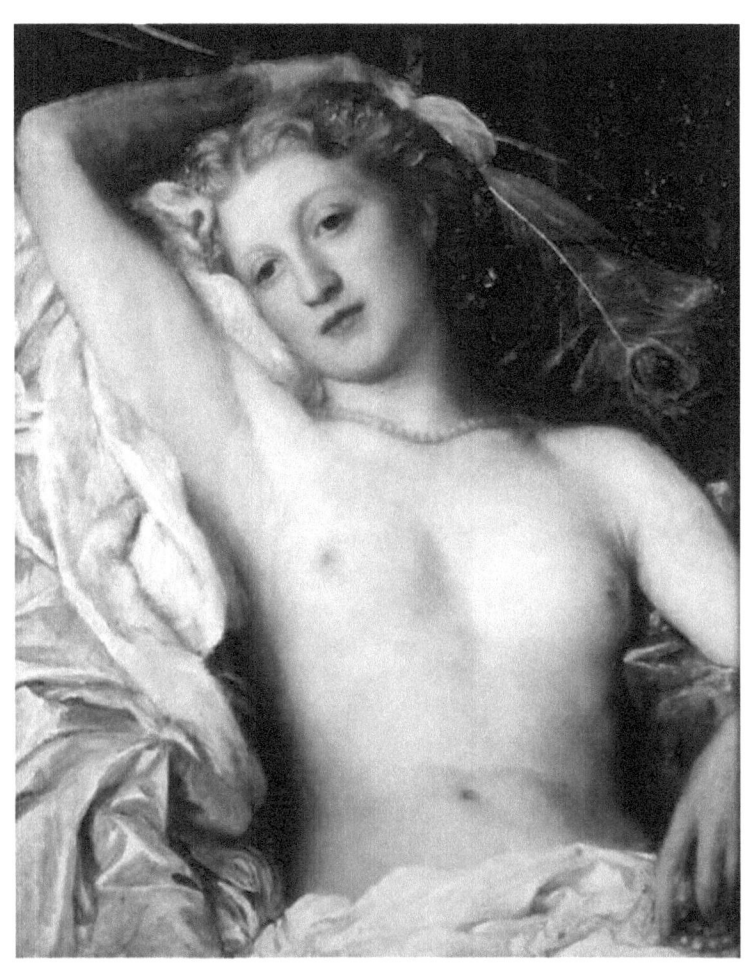

Girl with Peacock
Oil on canvas

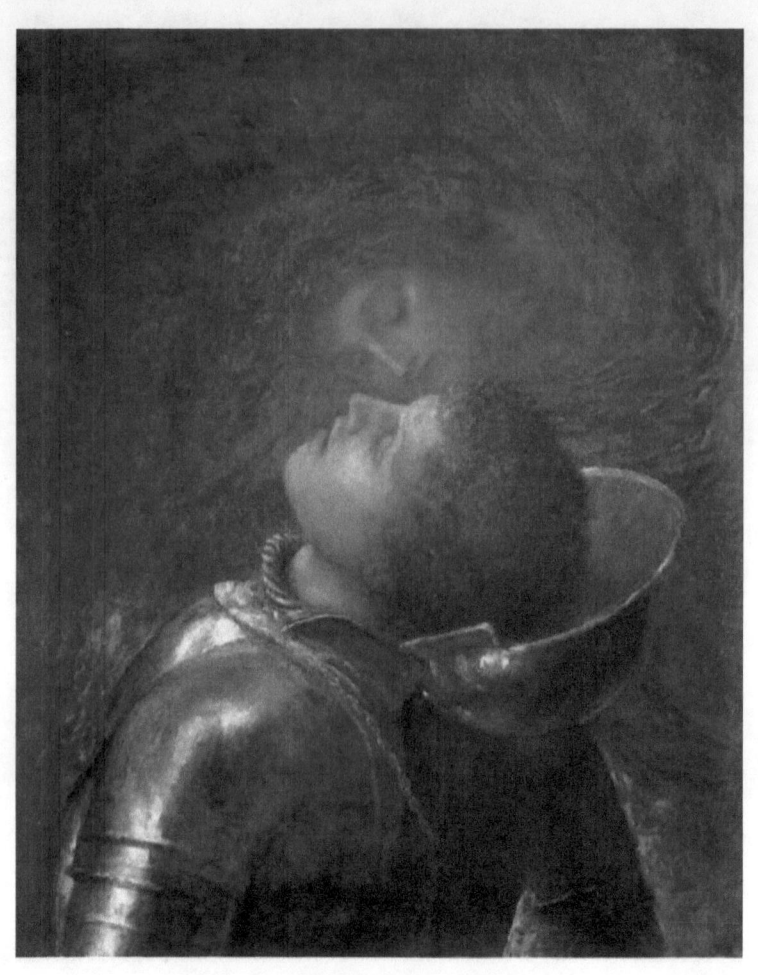

Happy warrior
Oil on canvas

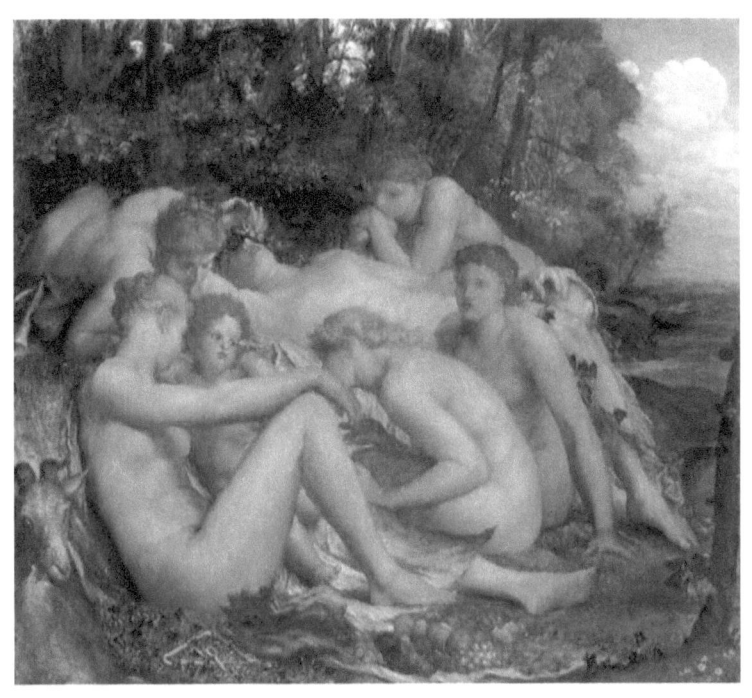

Infancy of Zeus
Oil on canvas

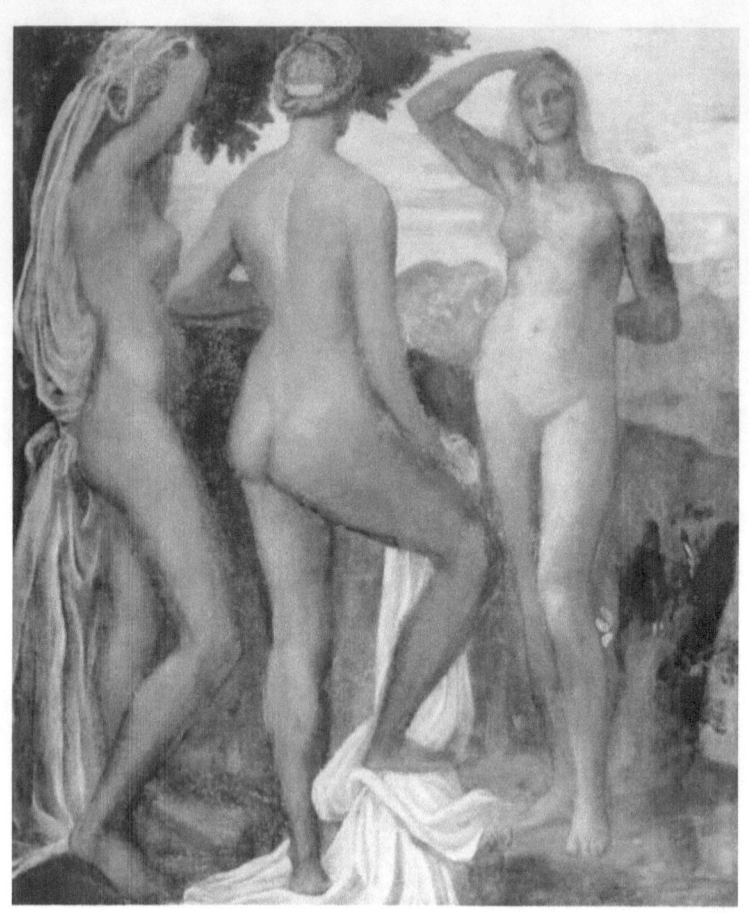

Judgement of Paris
Oil on canvas

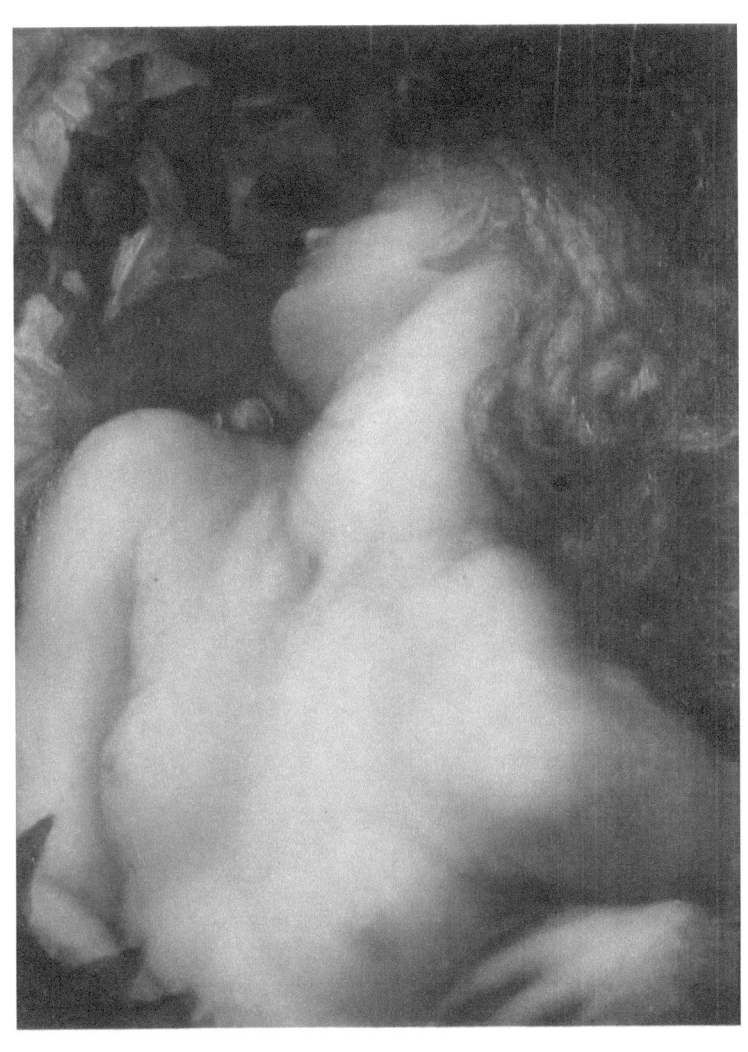

Klayti
Oil on canvas

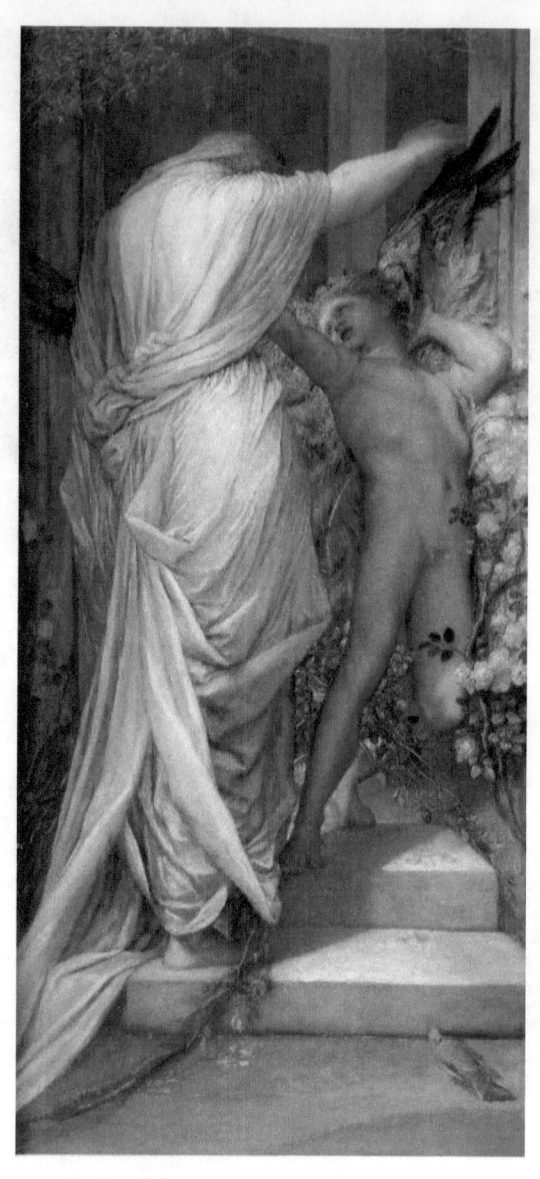

Love and Death
Oil on canvas

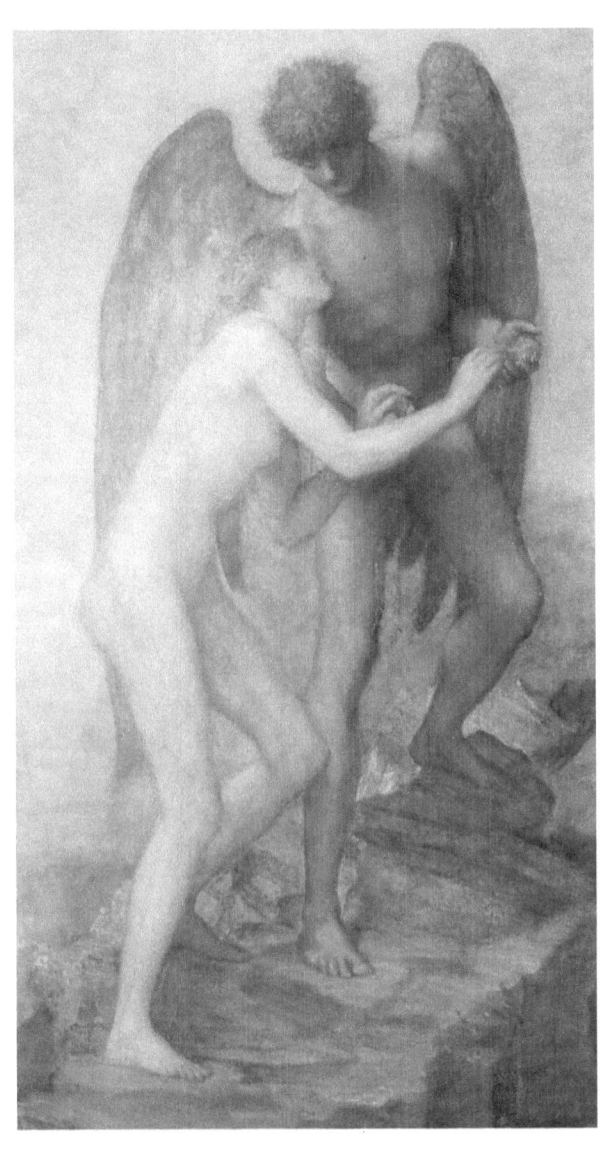

Love and Life
Oil on canvas

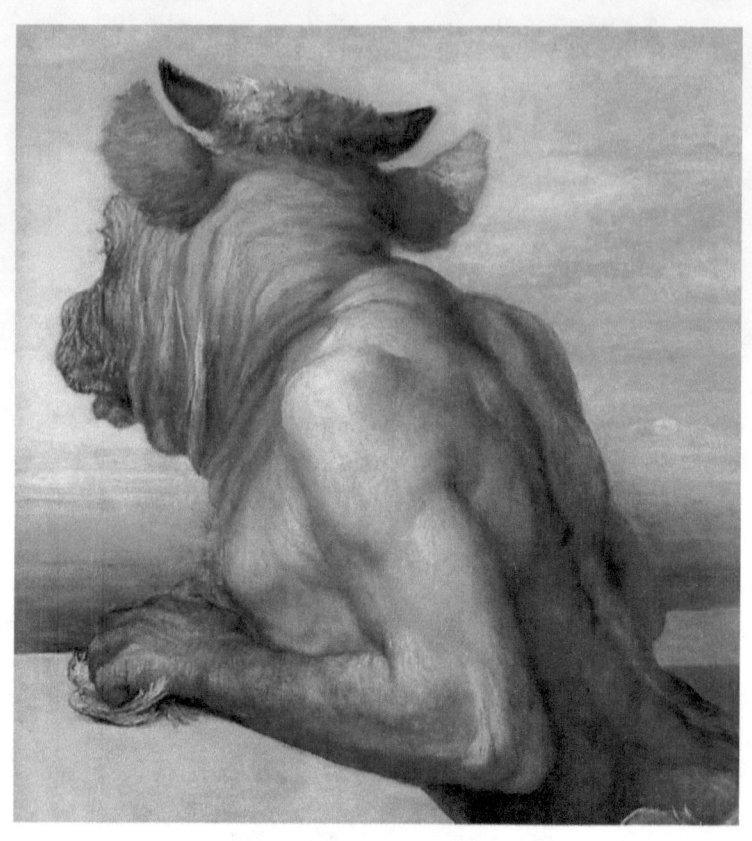

Minotaur
Oil on canvas

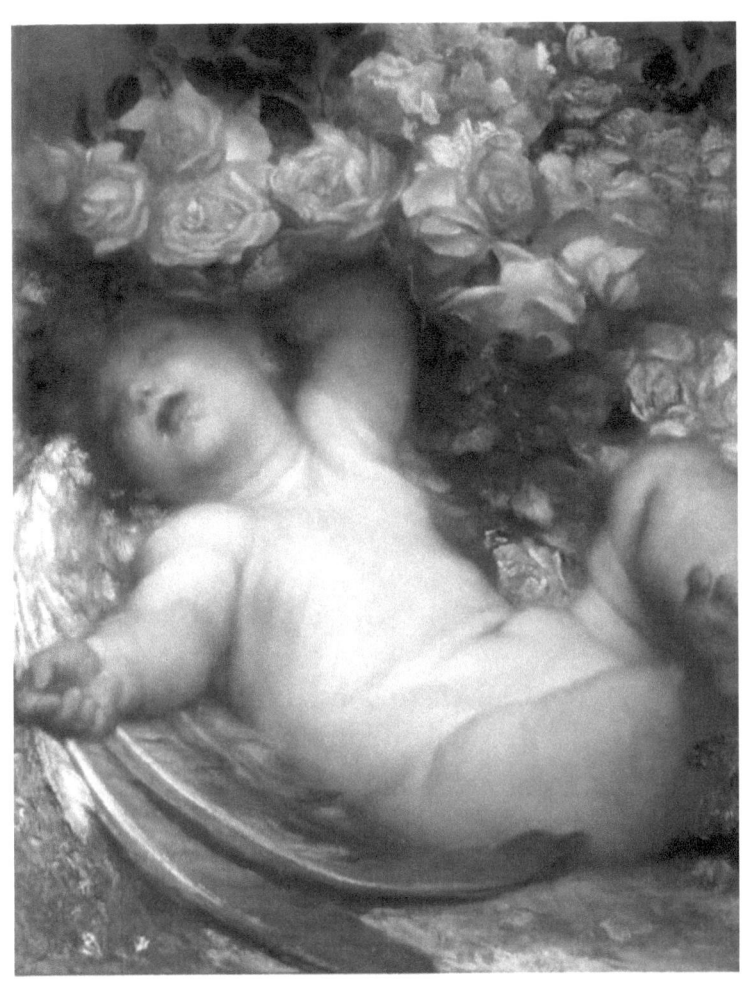

Cupid Asleep
Oil on canvas

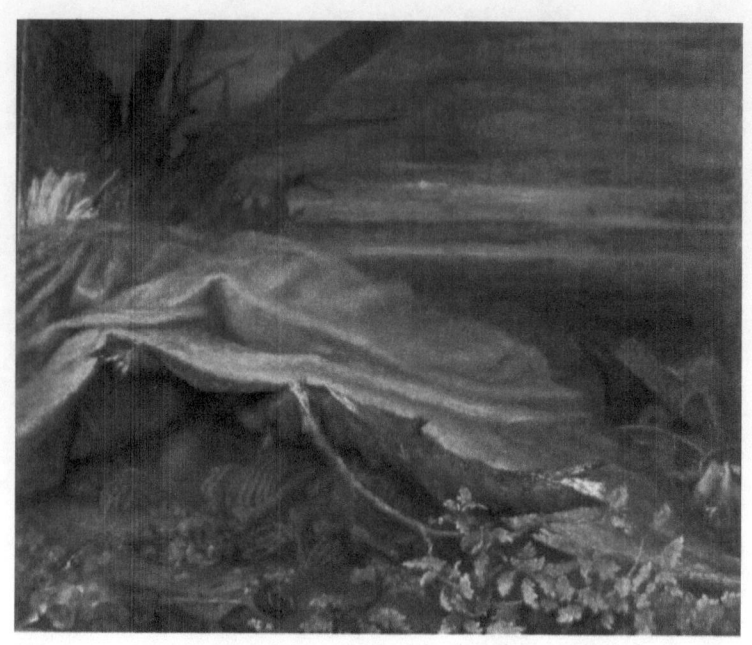

Can These Bones Live?
Oil on canvas

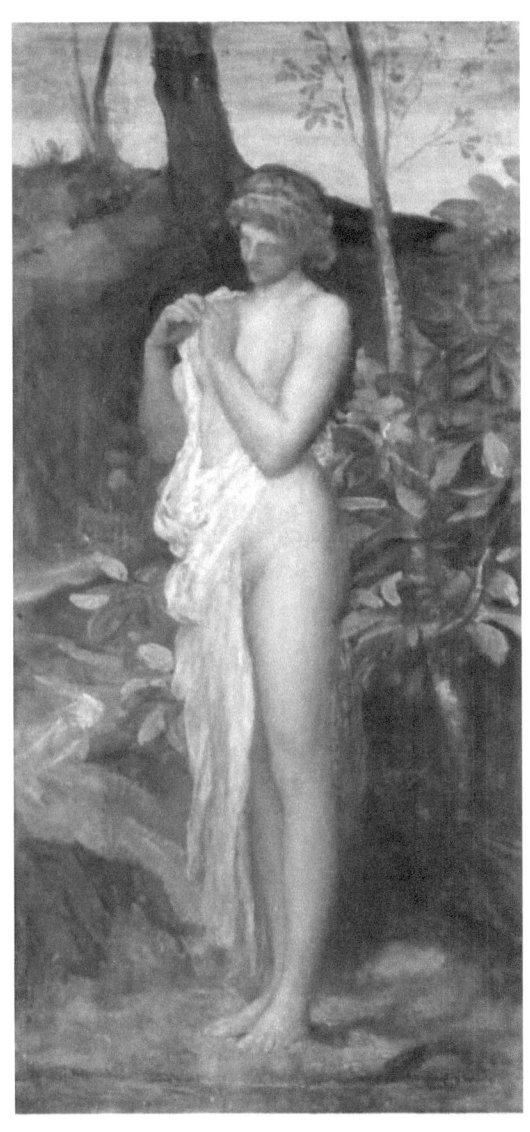

Daphne's Bath
Oil on canvas

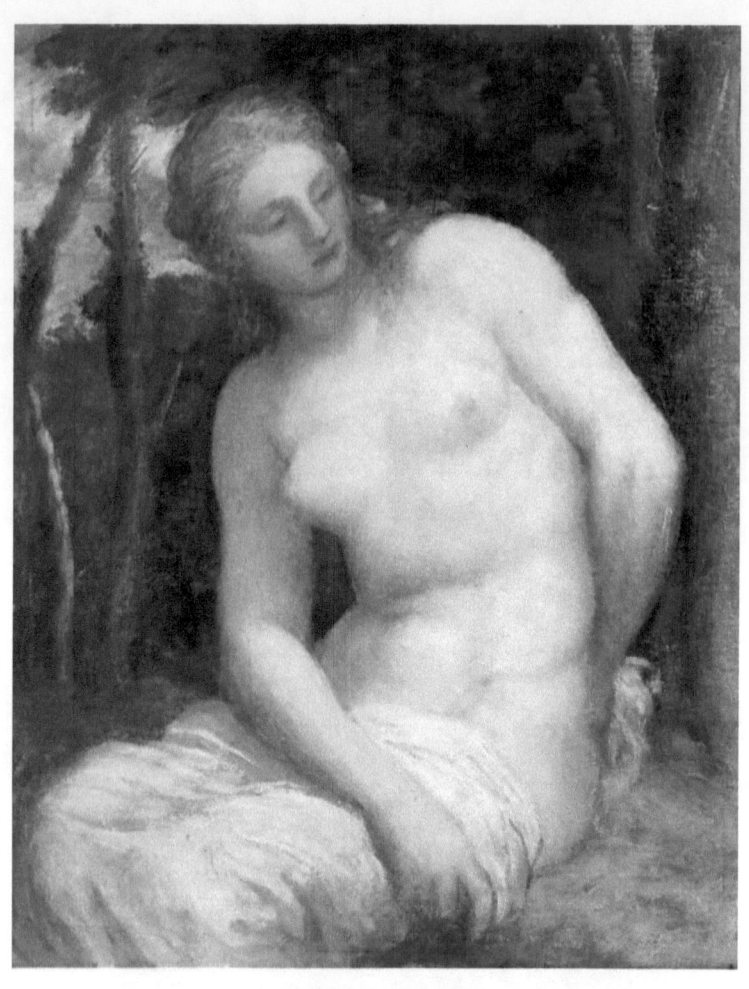

Daphne's Bath
Oil on canvas

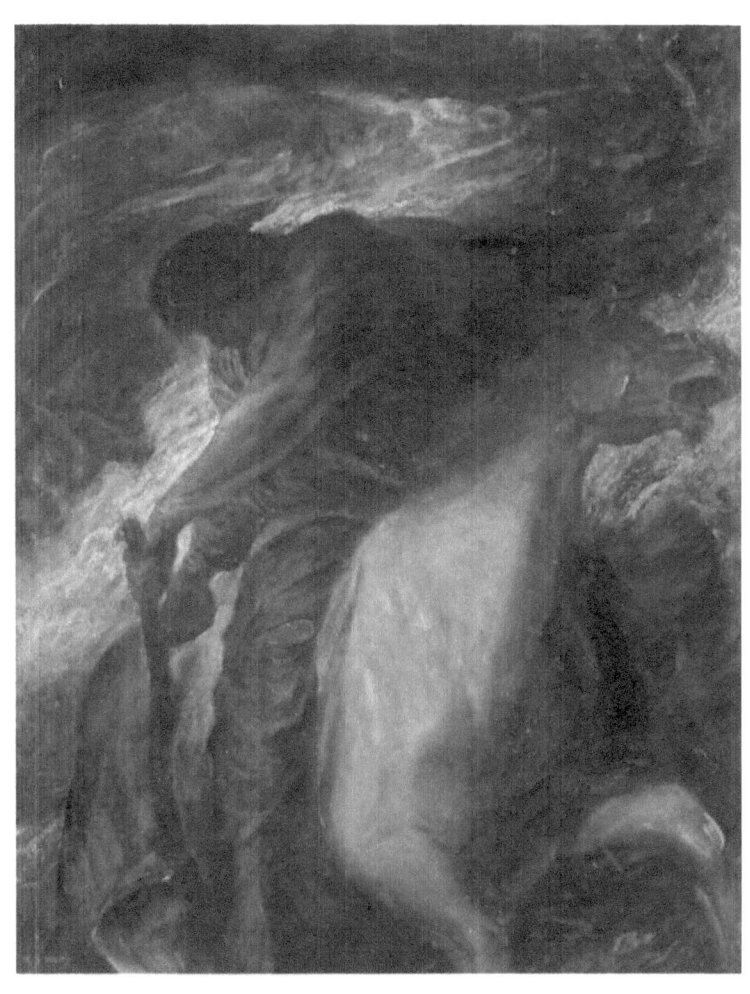

Death and the Pale Horse
Oil on canvas

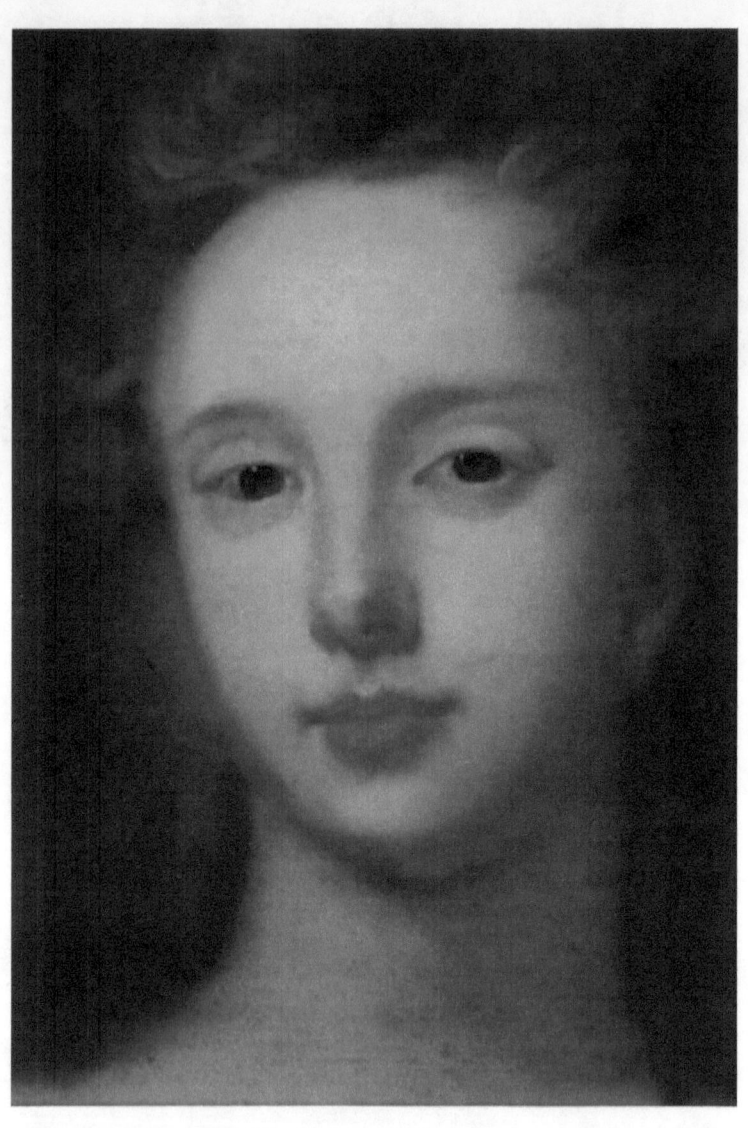

Early Copy from an Unidentified
Oil on canvas

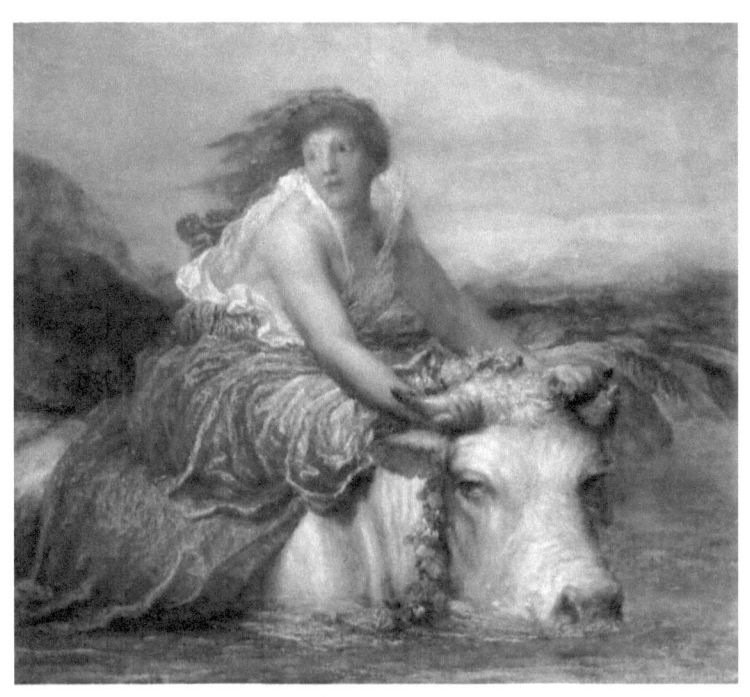

Europa
Oil on canvas

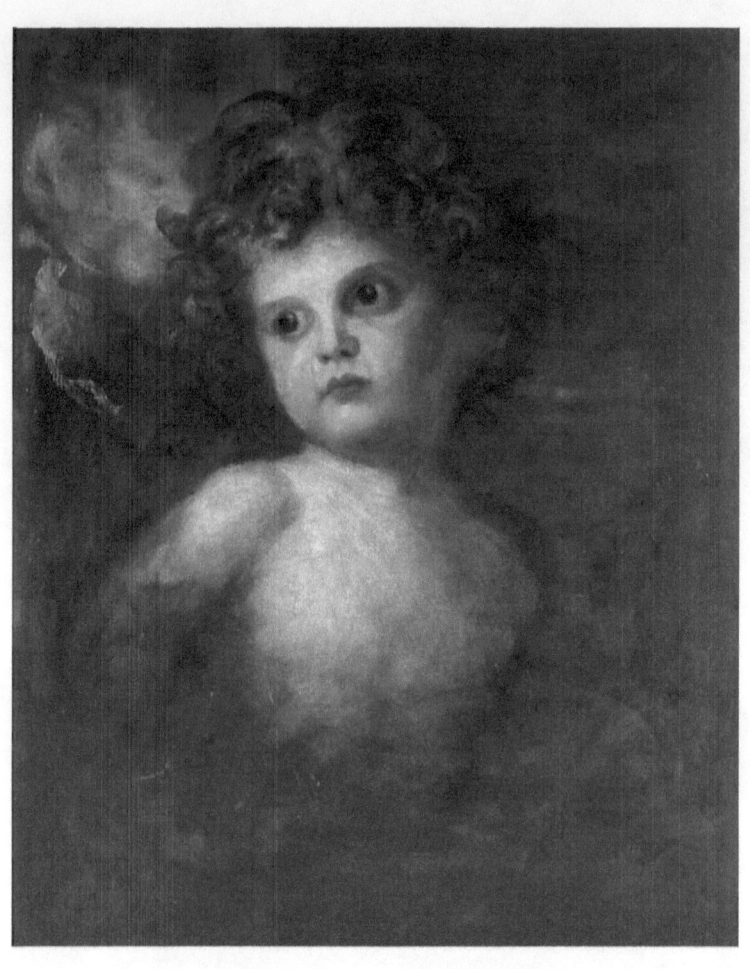

Ganymede (Son of Dr Zambaco)
Oil on canvas

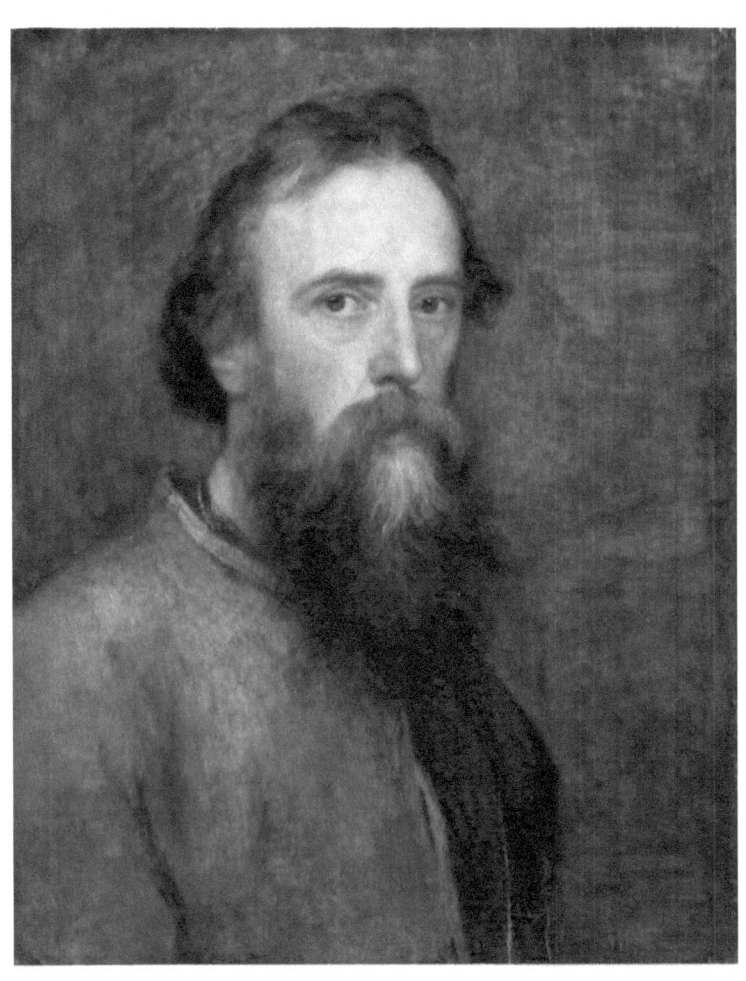

George Frederic Watts
Oil on canvas

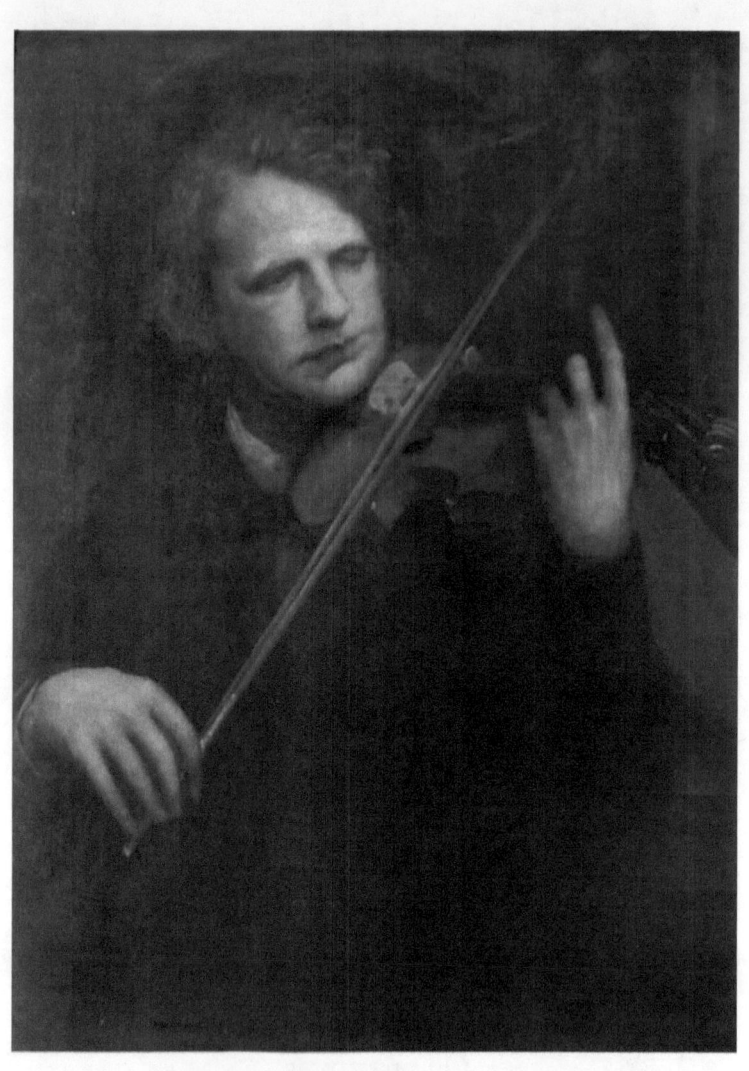

Dr J. Joachim
Oil on canvas

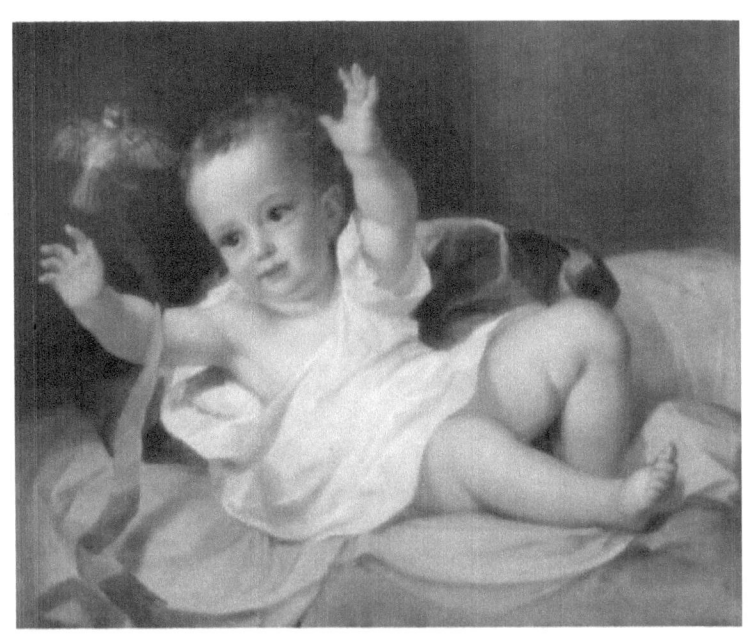

Gerald Hamilton as an Infant
Oil on canvas

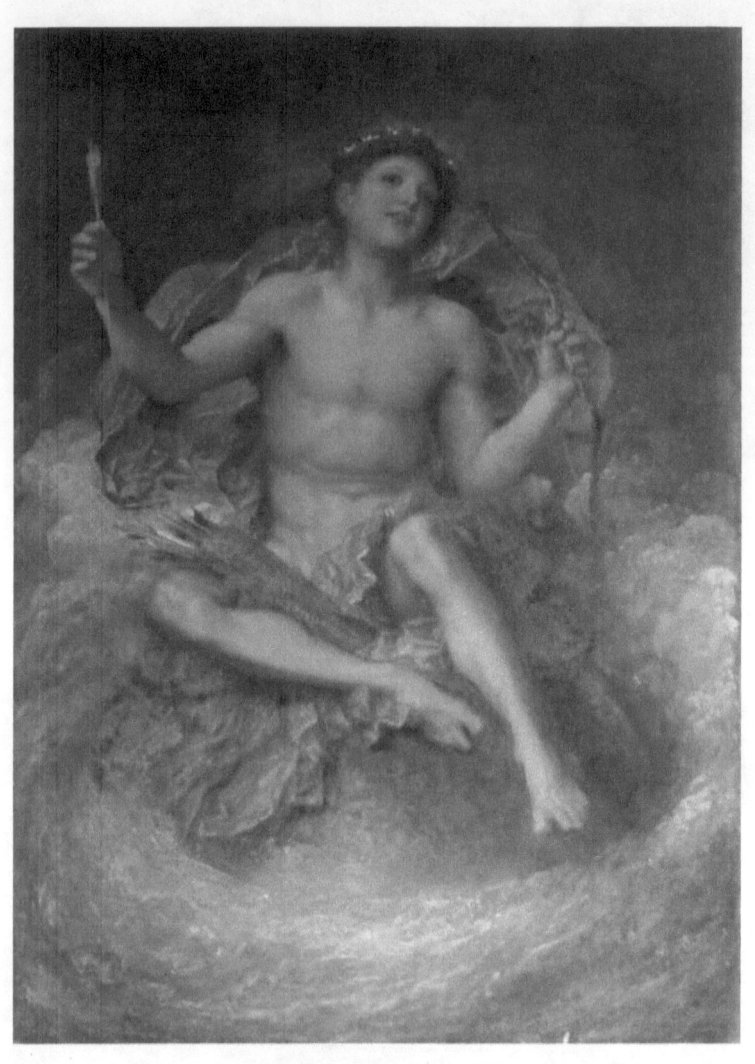

Idle Child of Fancy
Oil on canvas

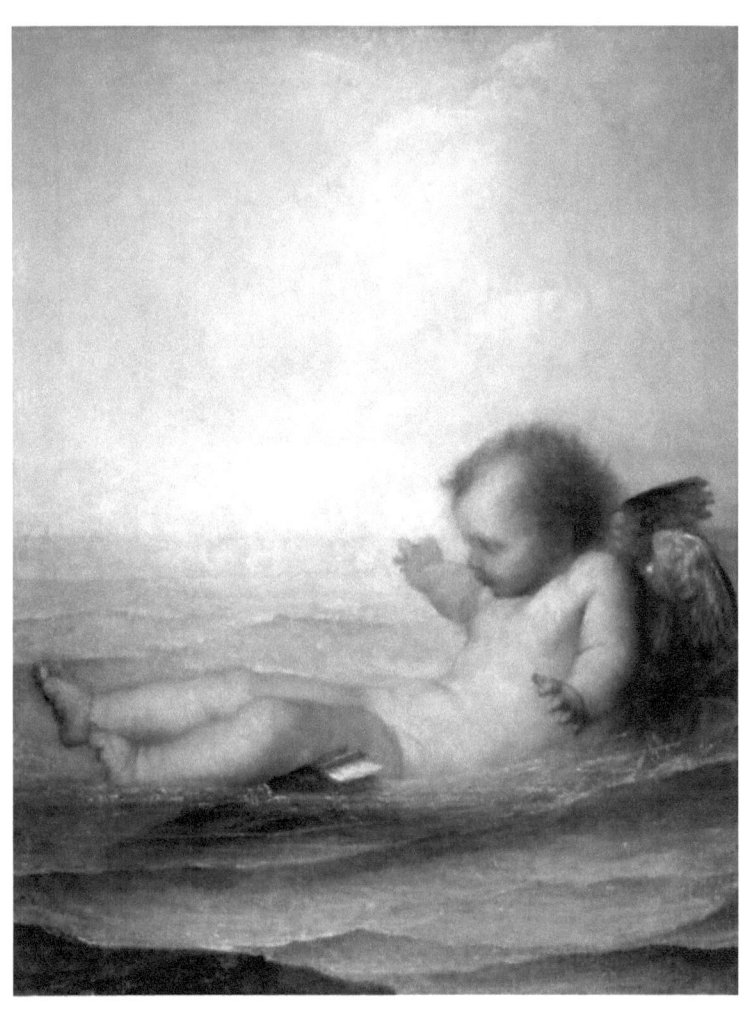

I'm Afloat
Oil on canvas

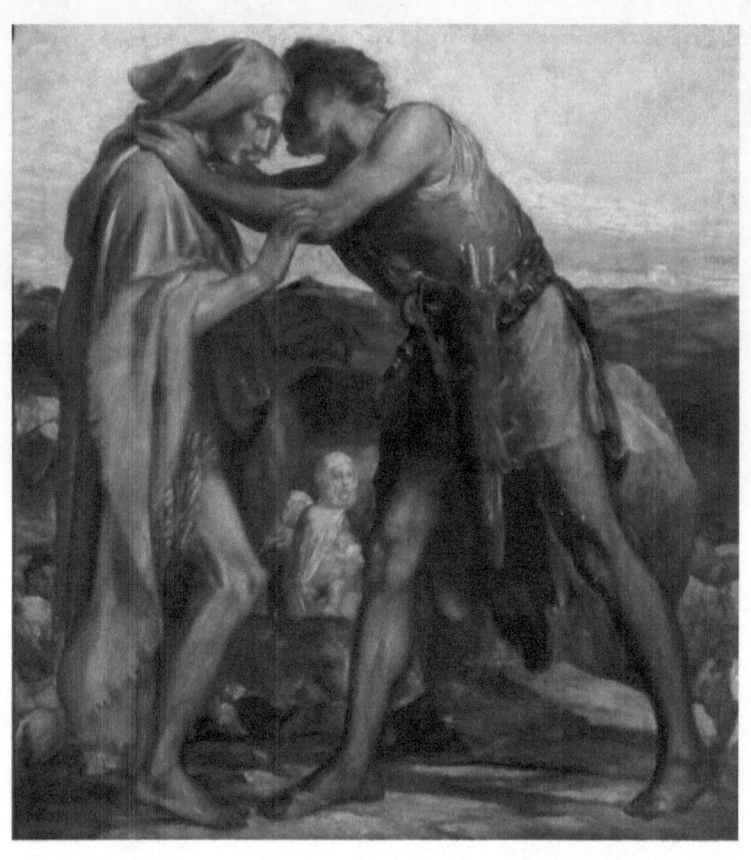

Jacob and Esau
Oil on canvas

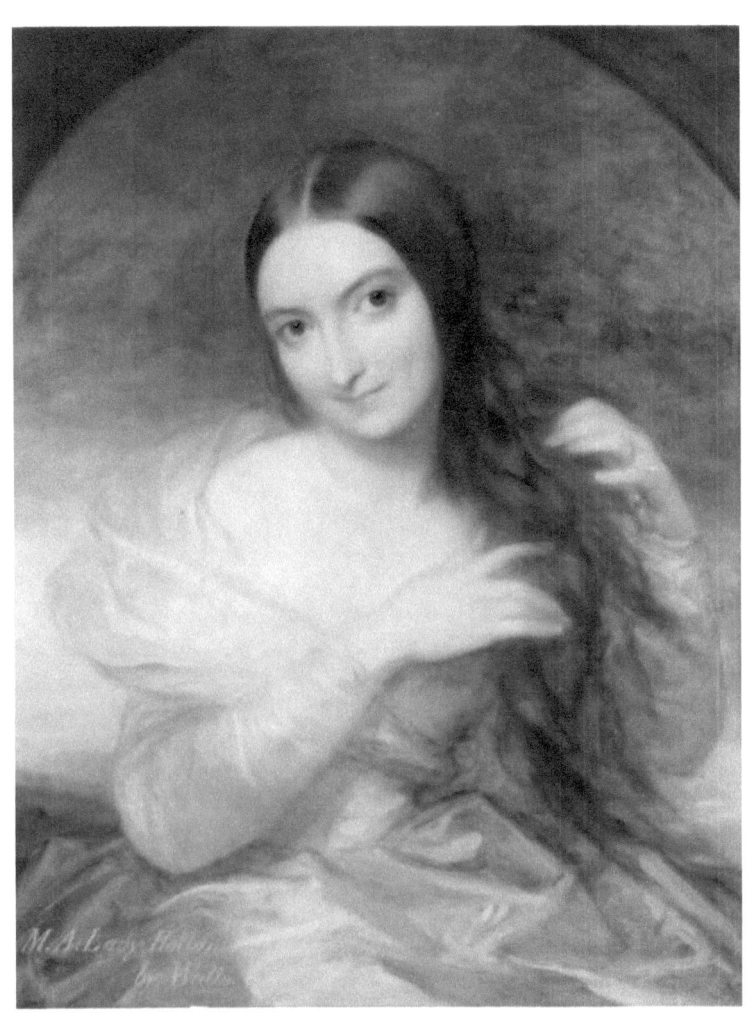

Lady Augusta Holland
Oil on canvas

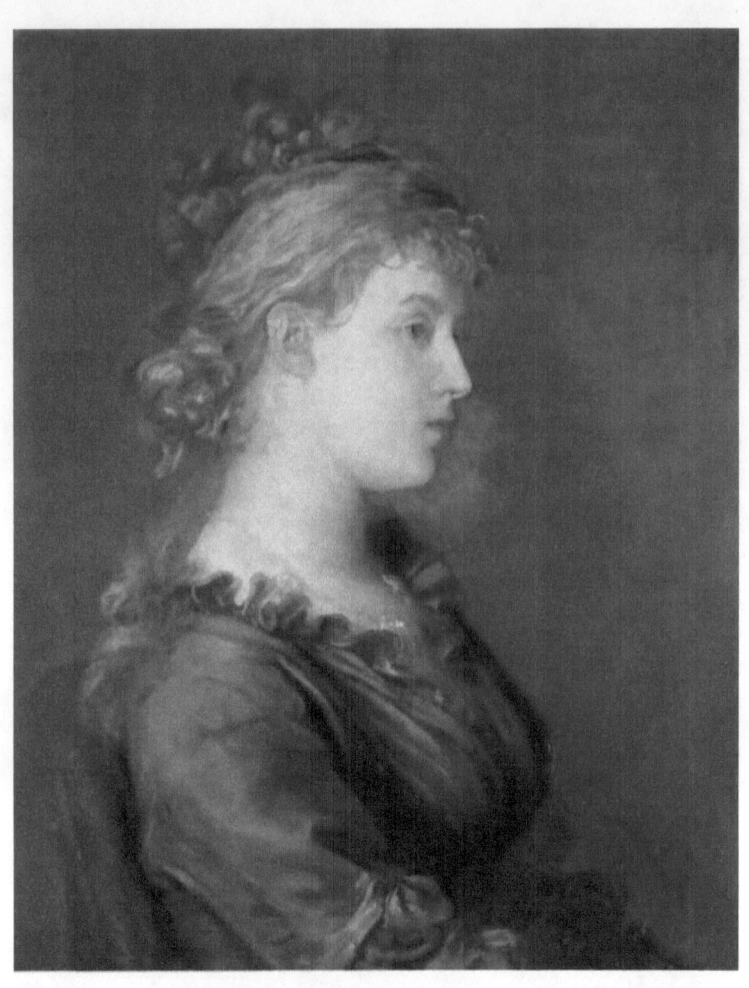

Lady Archibald Campbell
Oil on canvas

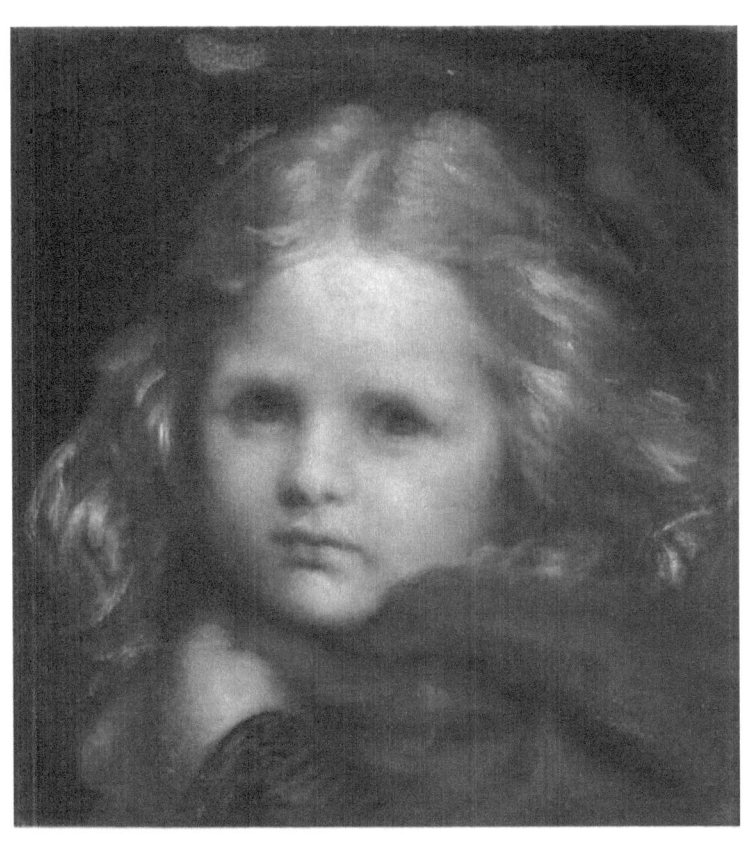

Little Red Riding Hood
Oil on canvas

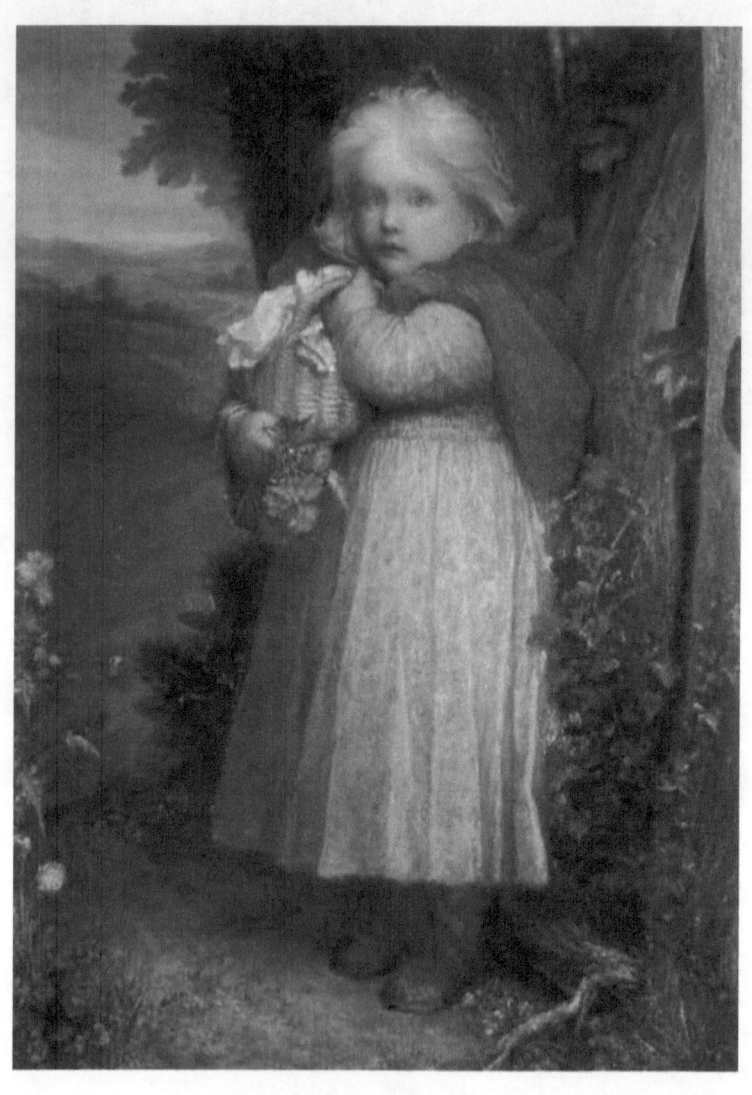

Little Red Riding Hood
Oil on canvas

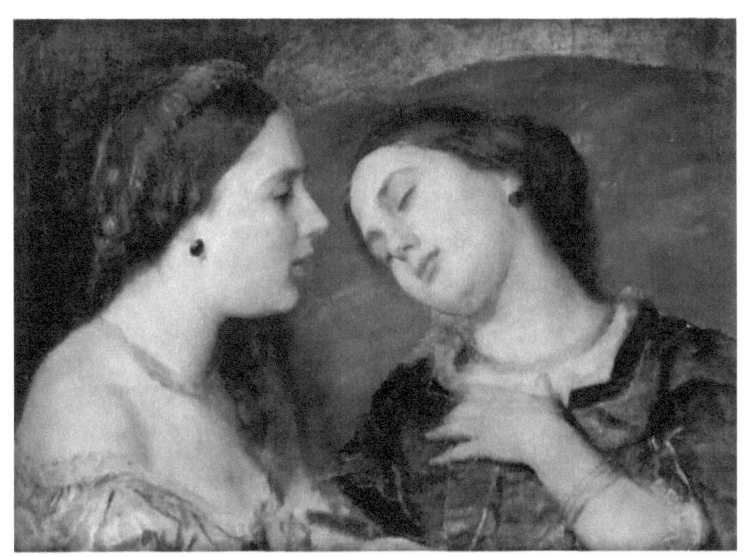

Miss Georgina Treherne
Oil on canvas

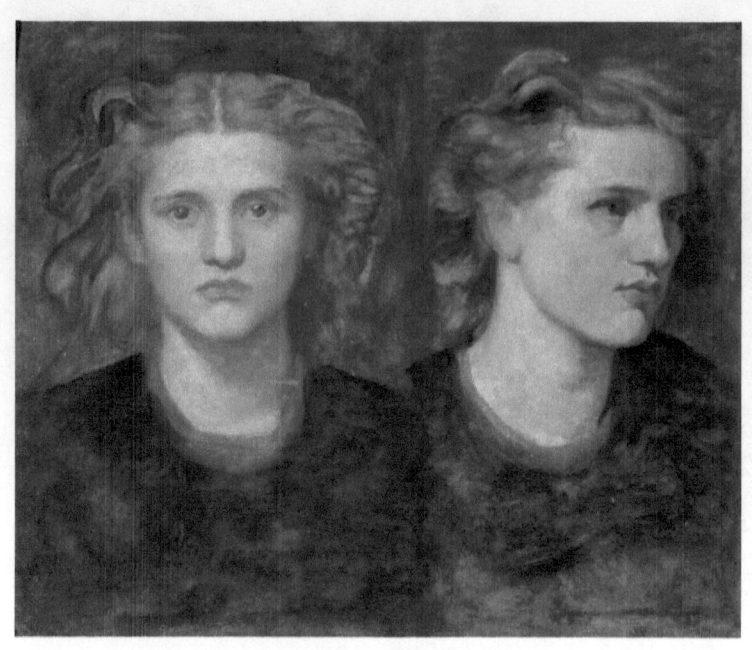

'Long Mary'
Oil on canvas

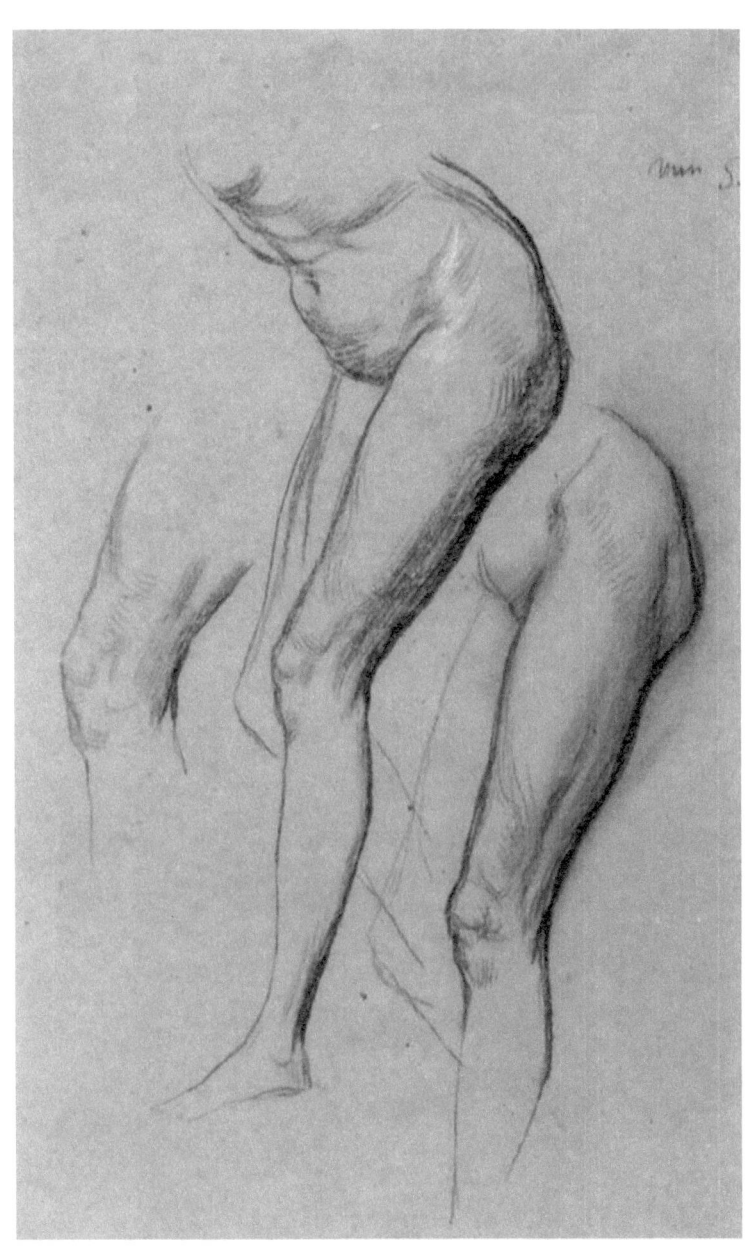

Nude Studies of Long Mary
Drawing

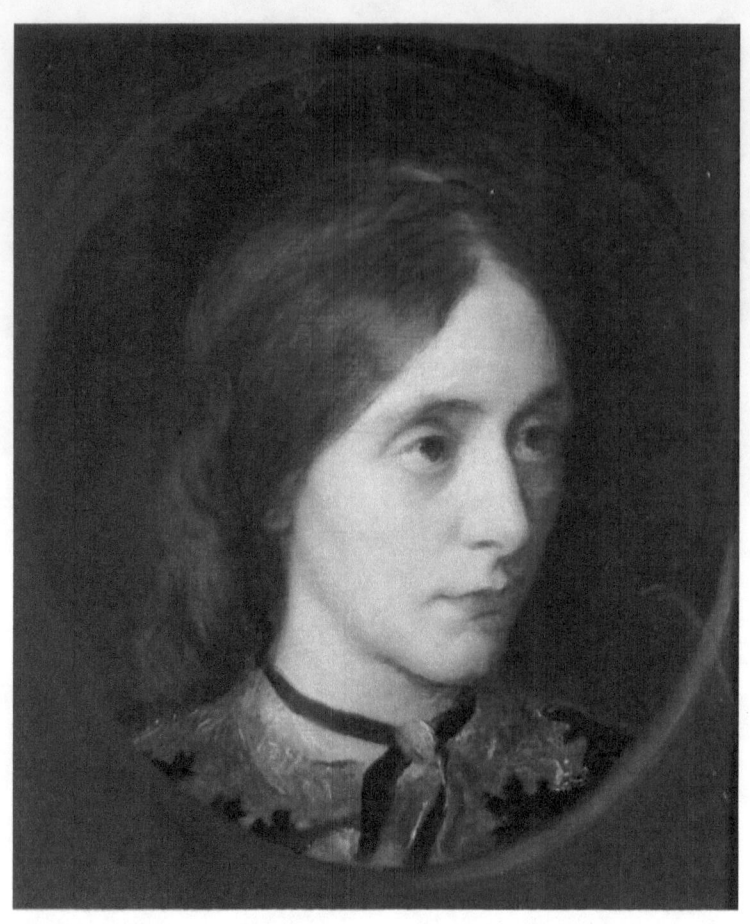

Mrs Morris
Oil on canvas

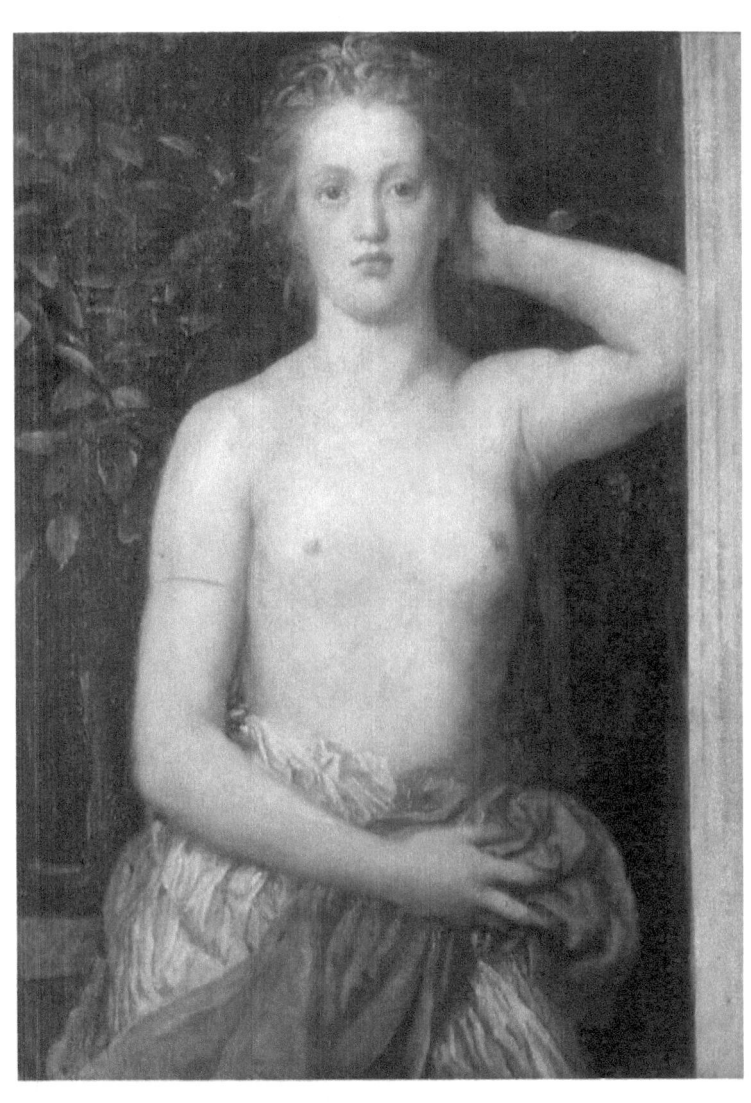

Rhodopis
Oil on canvas

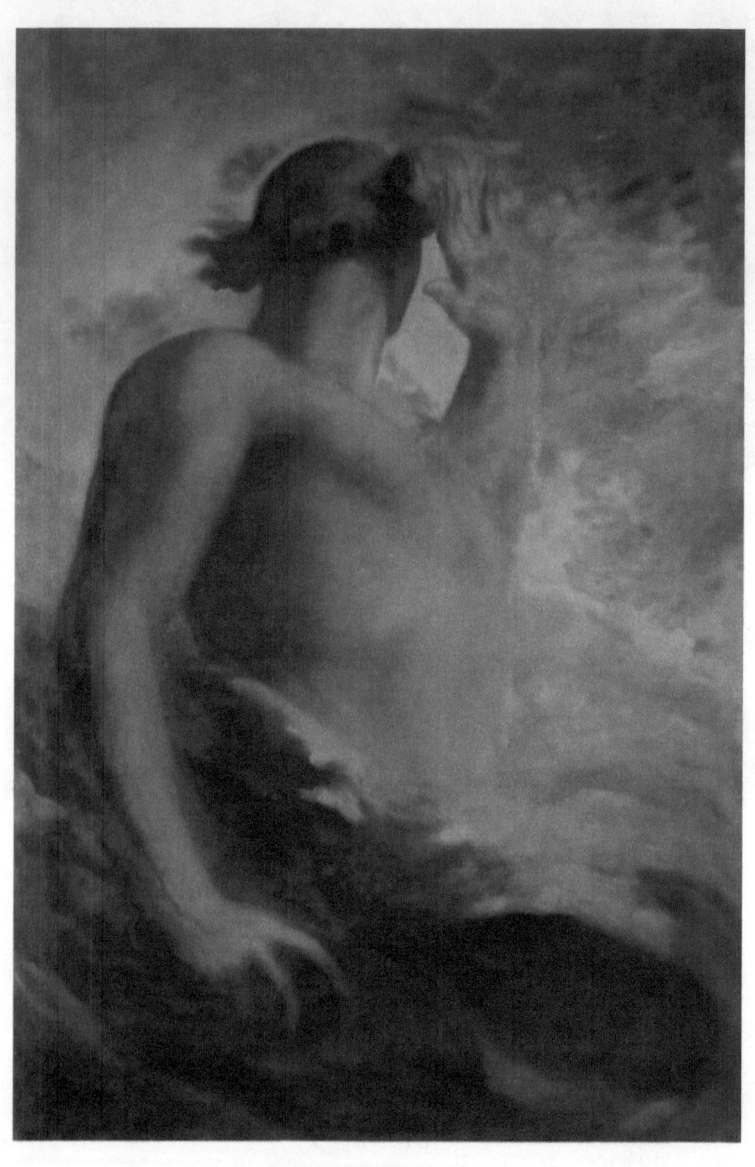

Satan
Oil on canvas

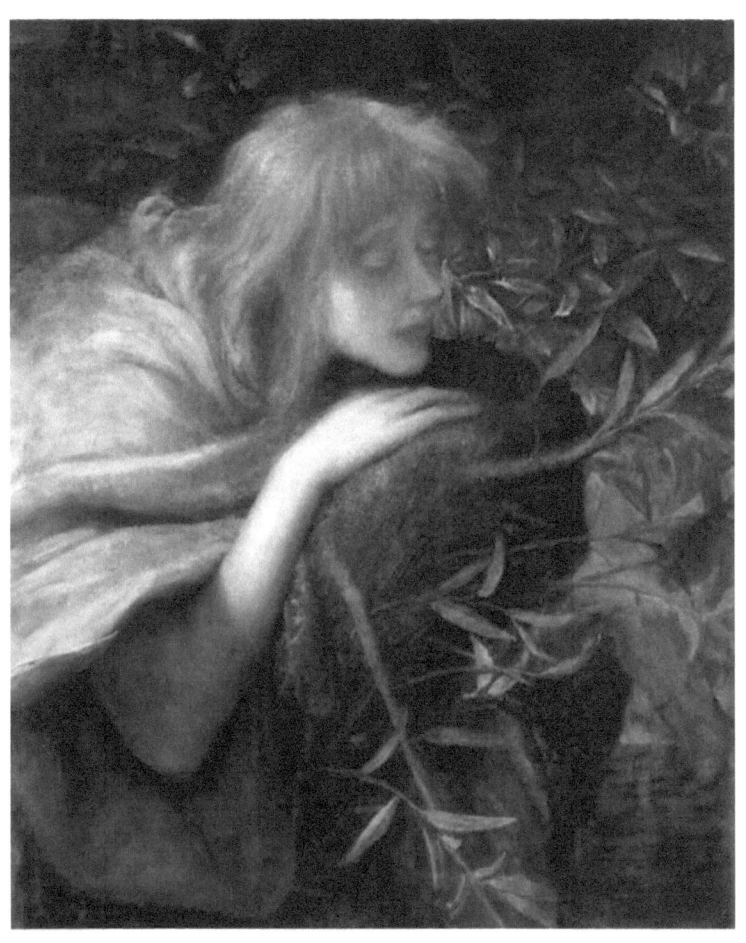

Ophelia
Oil on canvas

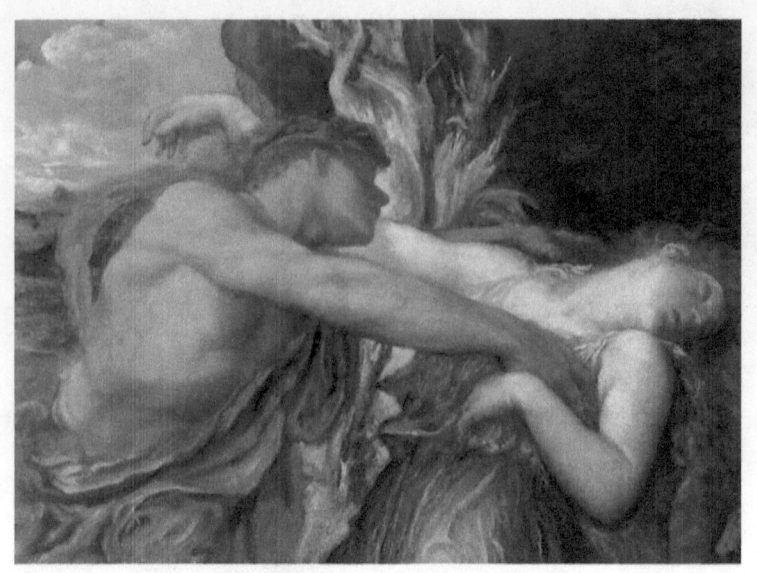

Orpheus and Eurydice
Oil on canvas

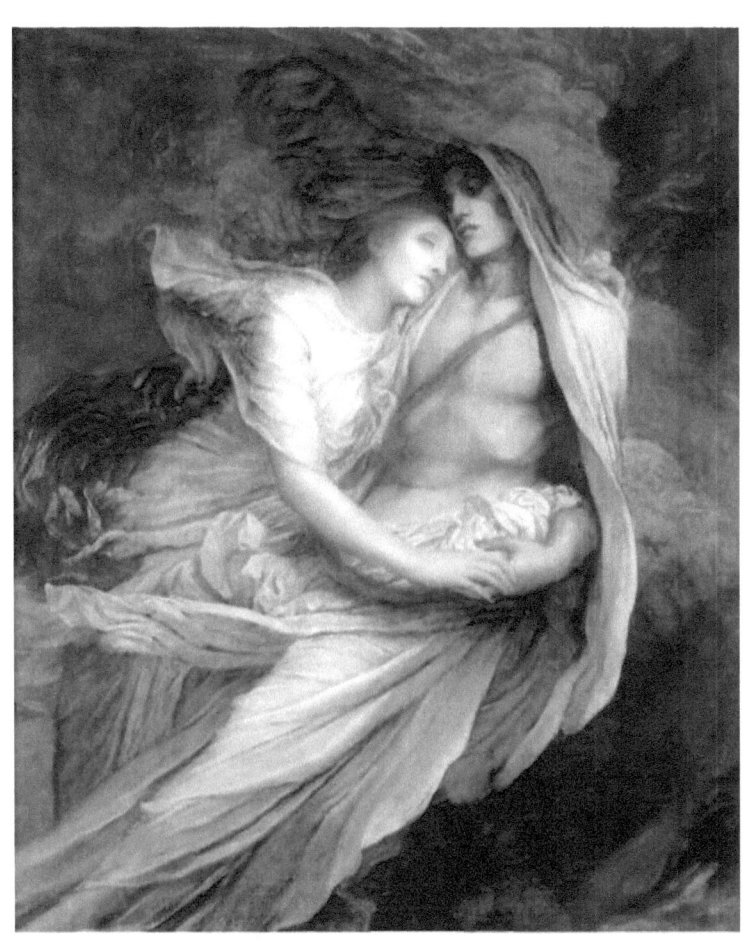

Paulo and Francesco
Oil on canvas

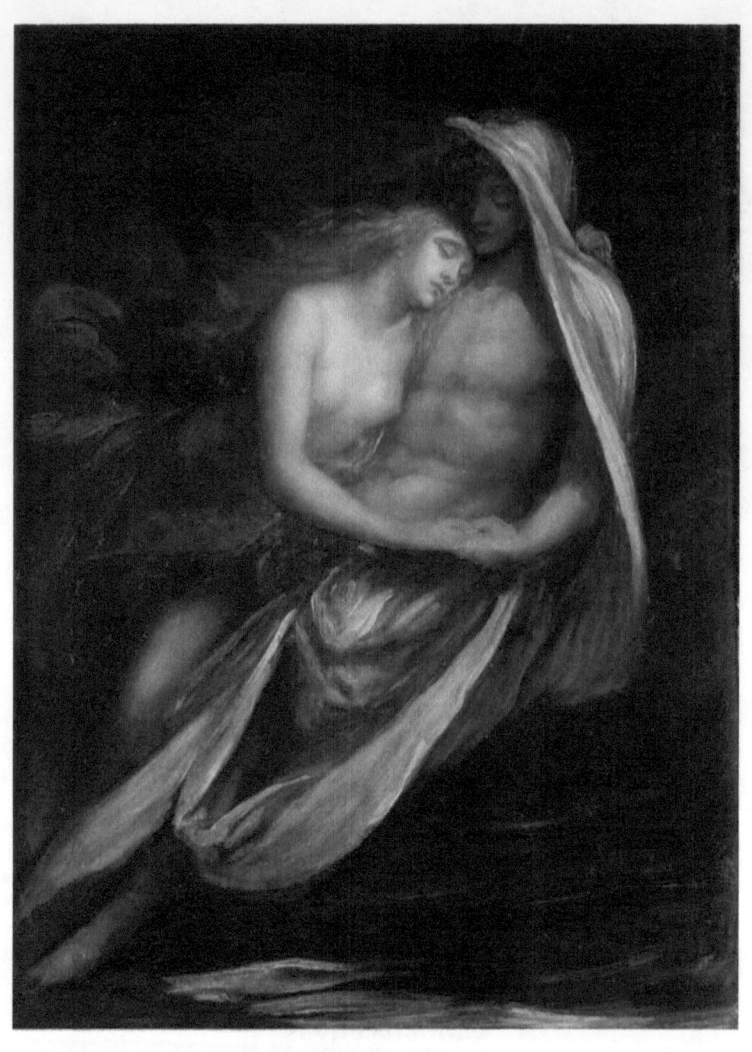

Paulo and Francesco
Oil on canvas

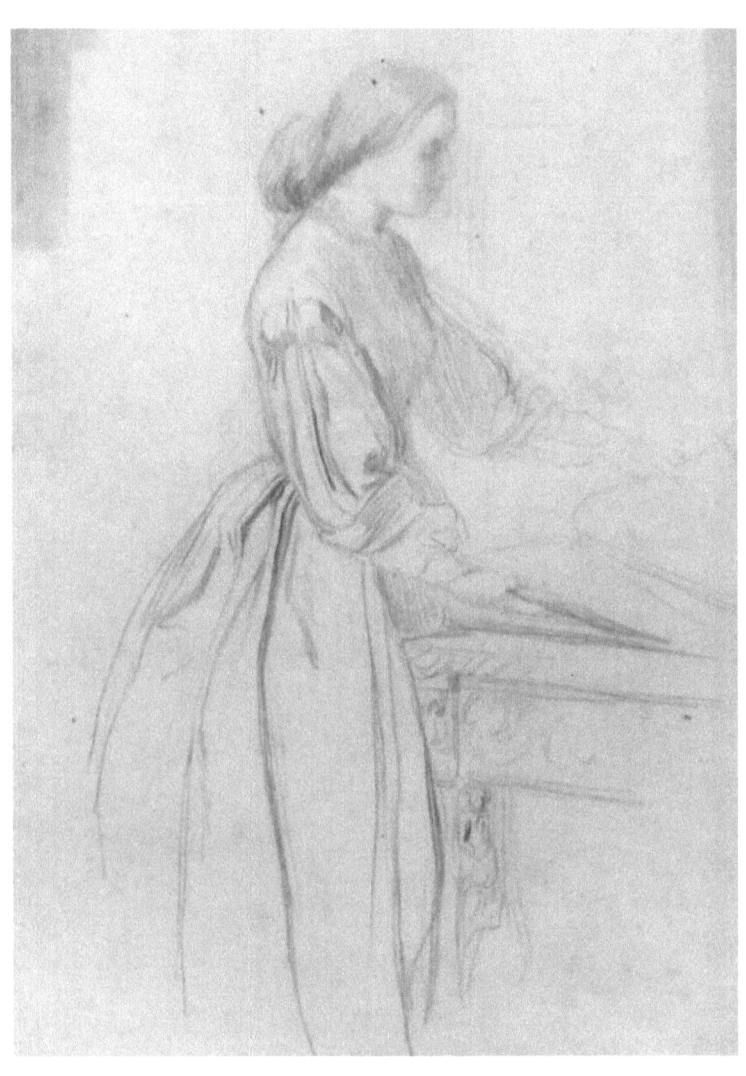

Portrait of a Lady, Possibly Julia Jackson
Drawing

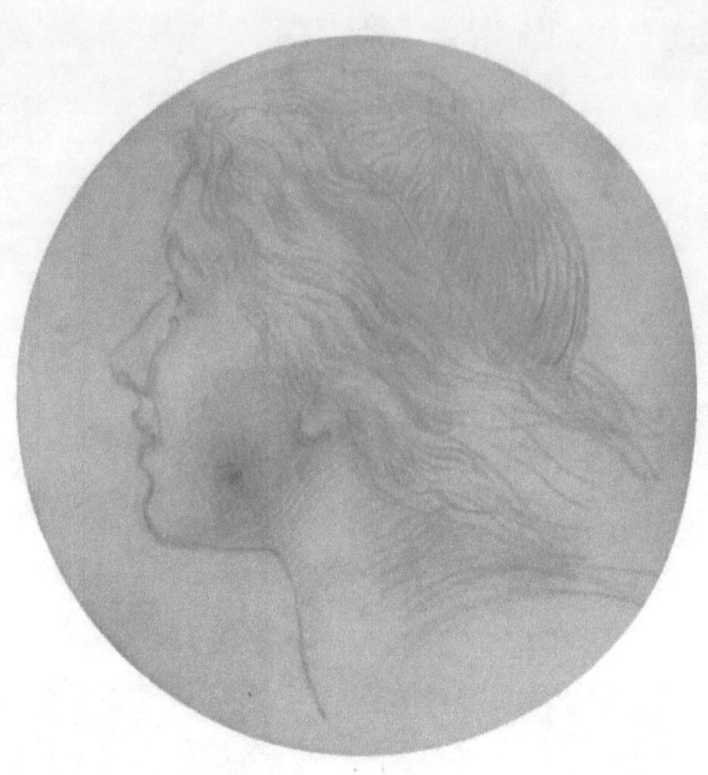

Portrait of Ellen Terry
Drawing

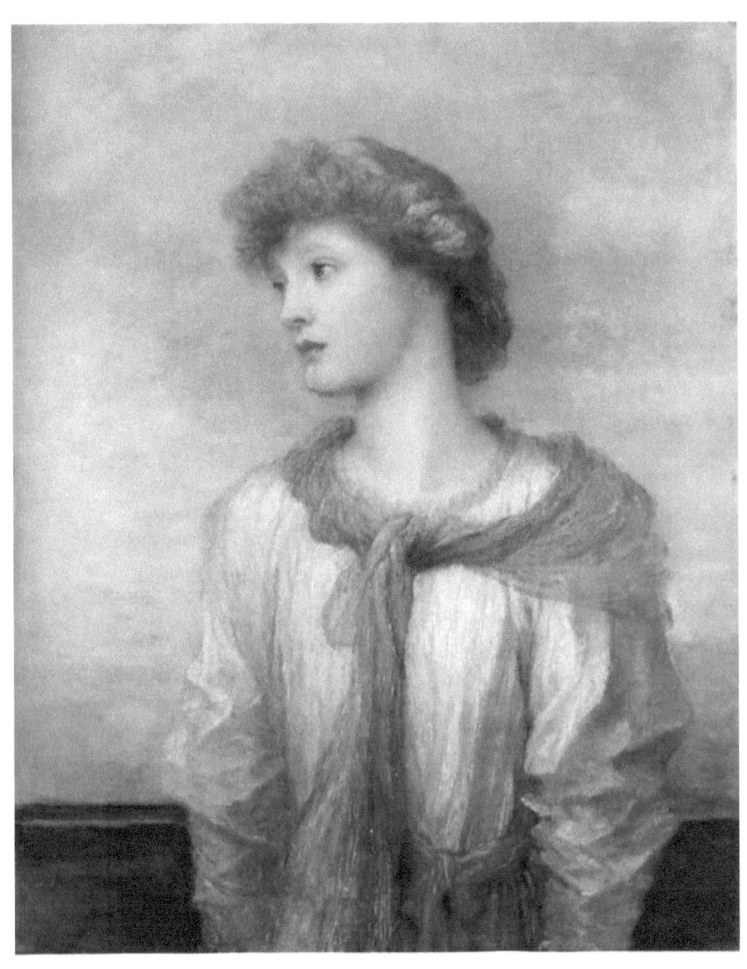

Portrait of Miss Lilian Macintosh
Oil on canvas

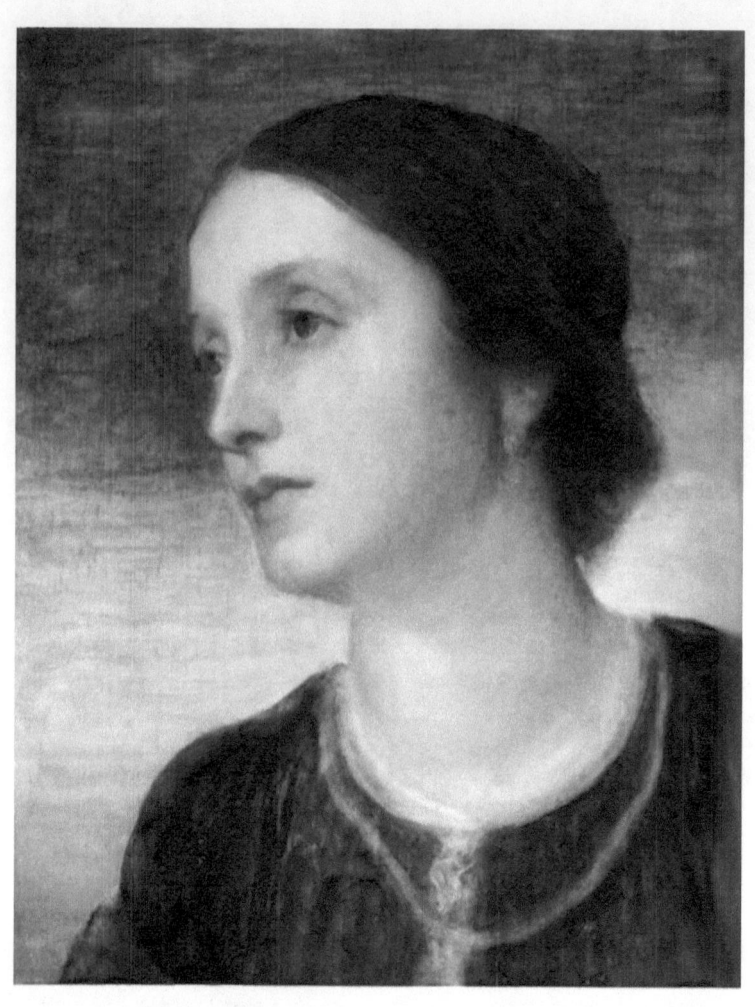

Portrait of the Countess Somers
Oil on canvas

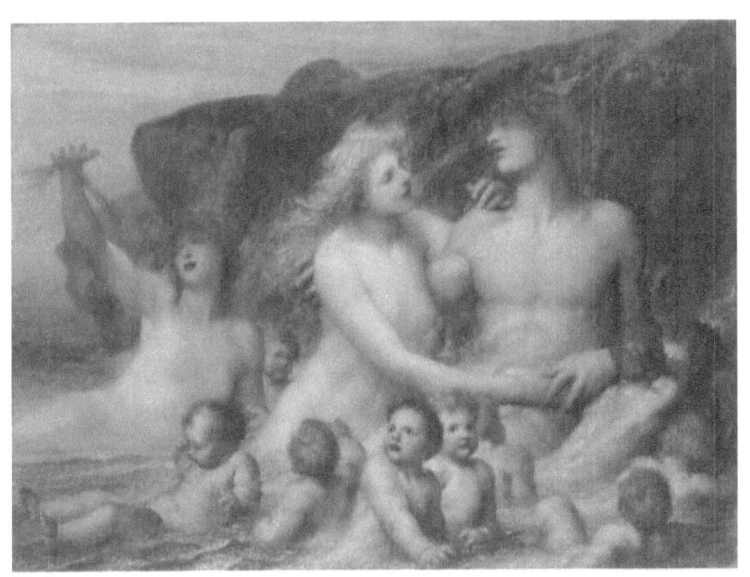

A Greek Idyll
Oil on canvas

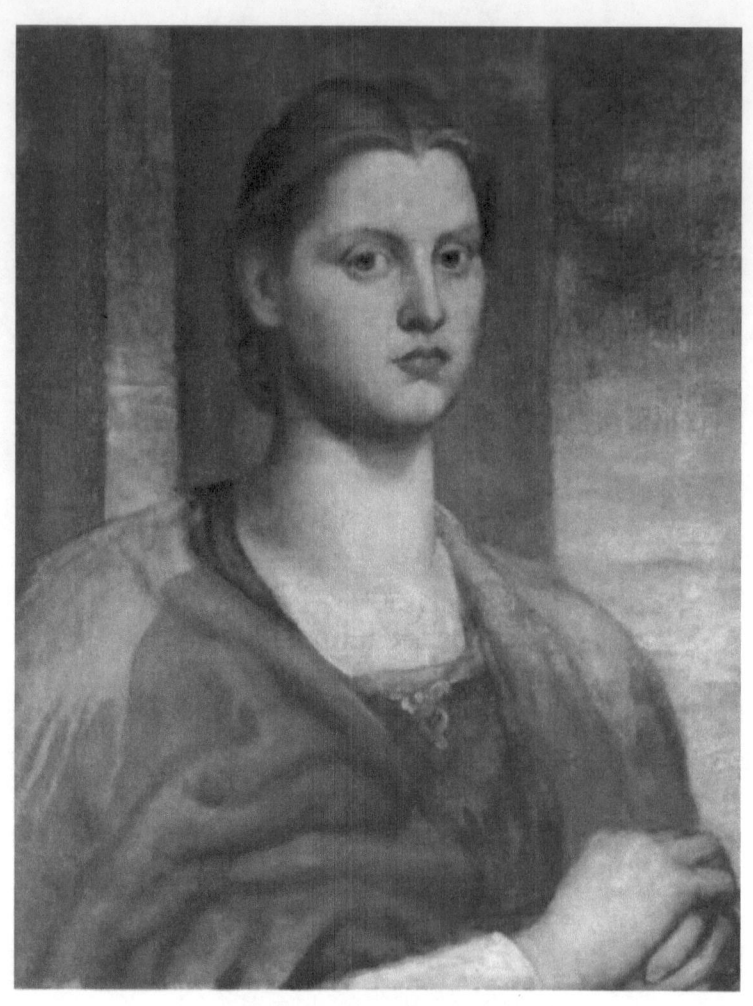

A Fair Saxon
Oil on canvas

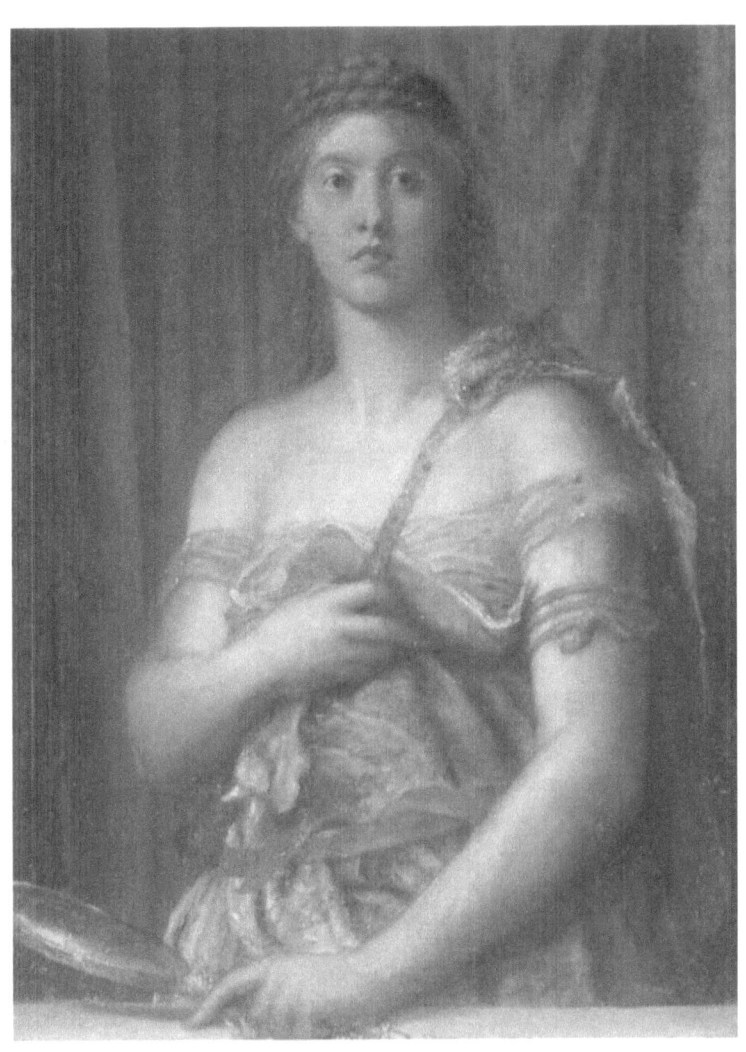

A Roman Lady
Oil on canvas

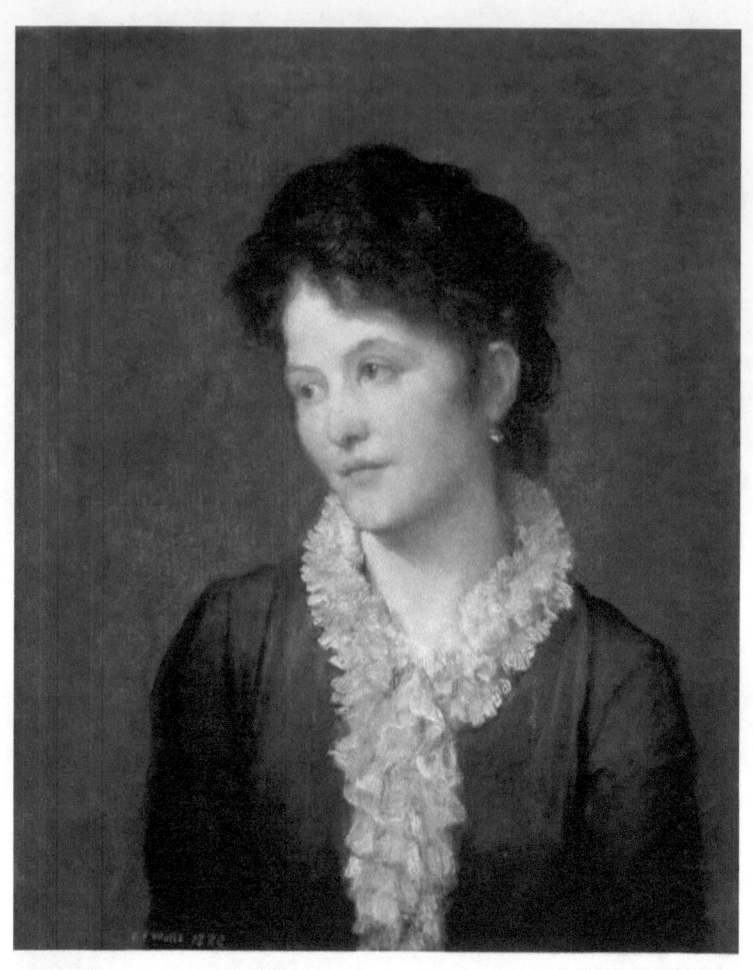

Agathonike Ionides
Oil on canvas

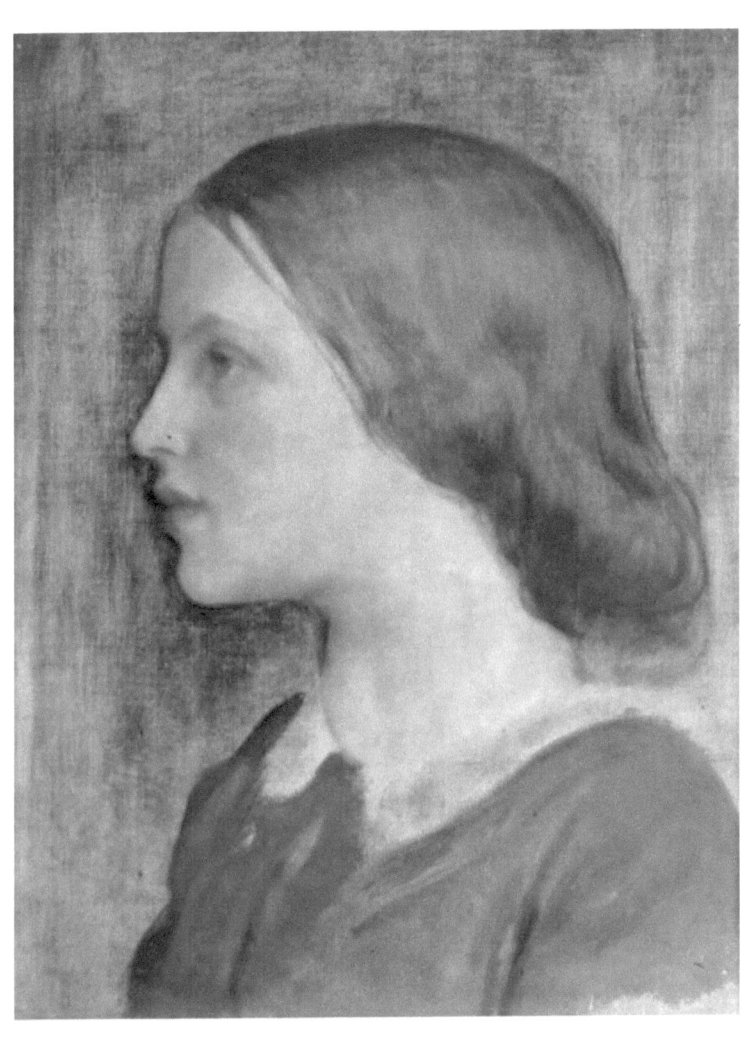

Aileen Spring-Rice
Oil on canvas

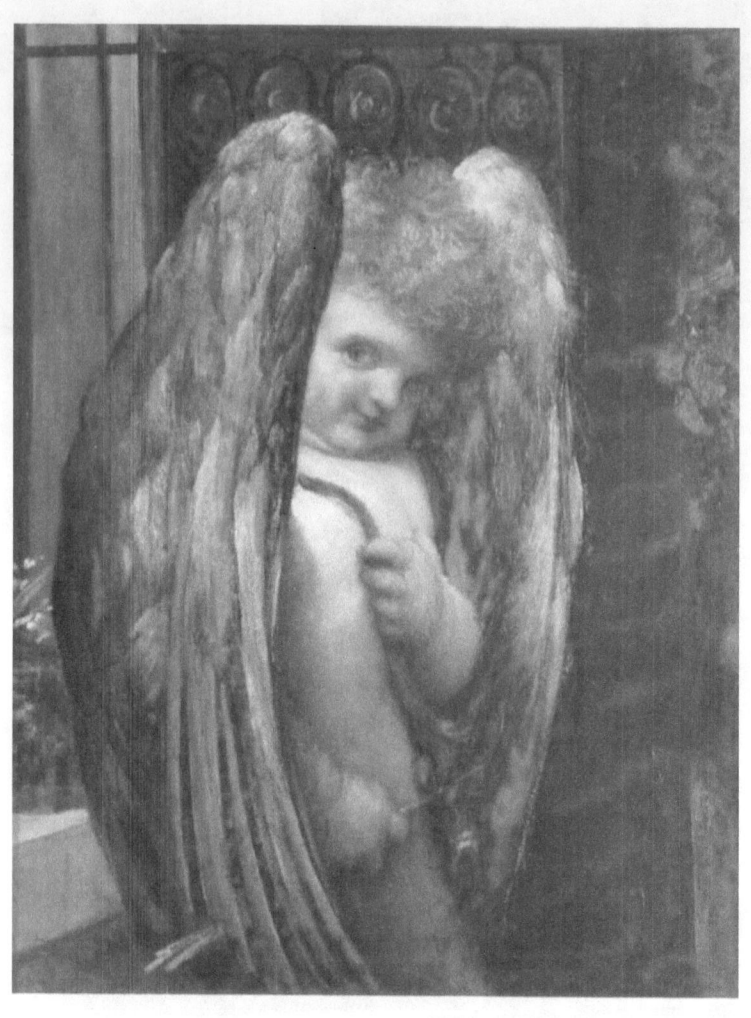

A Villain, I'll Be Bound
Oil on canvas

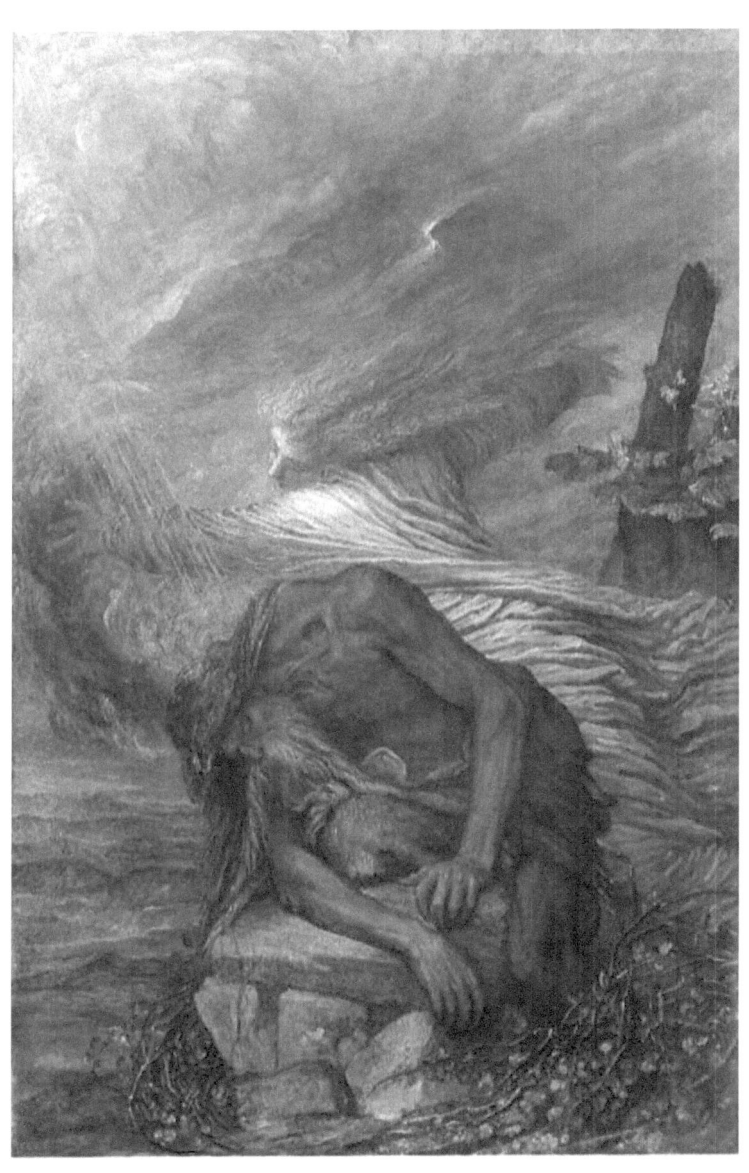

The death of Cain
Oil on canvas